Heritage Walks in south east Wales

Published by Sigma Leisure – an imprint of
Sigma Press, Stobart House, Pontyclerc, Penybanc Road
Ammanford, Carmarthenshire SA18 3HP

British Library Cataloguing in Publication Data

A CIP record for this book is available from the British Library

ISBN: 978-1-85058-935-8

Typesetting and Design by: Sigma Press, Ammanford, Carms

Maps: © Bute Cartographics

Photographs: © Rebecca Lees, except where noted

Cover photograph: above: Bwllfa Dare Terrace from the Penrhiwllech Trail © Rebecca Lees; below: Cyfarthfa Castle; photograph courtesy of Merthyr Tydfil County Borough Council

Printed by: TJ International Ltd, Padstow, Cornwall

Disclaimer: The information in this book is given in good faith and is believed to be correct at the time of publication. Care should always be taken when walking in hill country. Where appropriate, attention has been drawn to matters of safety. The author and publisher cannot take responsibility for any accidents or injury incurred whilst following these walks. Only you can judge your own fitness, competence and experience. Do not rely solely on sketch maps for navigation: we strongly recommend the use of appropriate Ordnance Survey (or equivalent) maps.

Heritage Walks in south east Wales

Rebecca Lees

For Ed

Preface

The walks in this book are diverse in length and landscape, yet they all have one thing in common; the rich history of south east Wales. From the world-class Blaenavon Heritage Site at the uppermost tip of the south Wales coalfields to the sweeping expanse of Cardiff Bay, the trails are centred on the vibrancy of Wales' past, with the aim of bringing back to life some of her most notable events and characters.

The fact that the walks are so varied reflects the story of the landscape. This corner of Wales is dominated by 'the valleys', carved out during the last Ice Age by glaciers moving south. Exploited in the industrial age for all they were worth, the valleys now lie exhausted, the legacy of that golden age still being paid. More prosperous are the cities; Cardiff continuing to reap the rewards of the 'Cool Cymru' tag attached at the end of the last millennium and, more recently, Newport, traditionally Cardiff's poor relation but recently vying for the limelight with events such as the Ryder Cup and groundbreaking archaeological discoveries at Caerleon. Although the trails included here are undoubtedly weighted towards the industrial era, which inspired the author Alexander Cordell to produce such classics as *Rape of the Fair Country* and *The Fire People*, the features and landmarks along the way span 2,000 years, the age of iron and coal bookended by the Romans' great forts and the relics of post-war optimism.

Wales has been eyed up by invaders time and time again, with south-east Wales a particular strategic target. In the first century it was the Romans who marched in and subjugated the indigenous Silures; after the Battle of Hastings it was the Normans, wrestling control from the powerful lords and stamping their authority on the church. The same could be said of the iron and coal masters who came later; predominantly Englishmen who bought up great swathes of mineral-rich land and reaped the profits of back-breaking Welsh labour. Charcoal furnaces had existed in south Wales since the 1500s but iron-making was not a major industry until the early 19th century. When it finally arrived, however, its scale was astonishing. Rural communities were quickly swallowed as ironworks churned up the landscape and workers poured in from England, Ireland, Spain and Italy in the hope of better prospects. In 1770, Wales' population stood at less than half a million; by 1851 this had more than doubled.

At the centre of this was Merthyr, the largest town in Wales by 1841. By this time south Wales was producing 40% of Britain's pig iron output and exporting it via a criss-cross of canals leading to the ports of Newport, Cardiff and Swansea. But it was the coming of the railways which drove the revolution in Wales to its peak. Their start was slow, despite the promise of Richard Trevithick's inaugural steam journey from Penydarren. Yet the pace, once gathered, was unstoppable, allowing coal to overtake iron production and turning the valleys into a network of tracks, viaducts and bridges heavy with the signature of one Isambard Kingdom Brunel.

Some of these landmarks are today among the most popular on the Welsh tourism trail; others are tucked away and barely discovered by those living on their very doorstep. This book explores these locations via a mix of challenging hikes across rough countryside and gentler town trails, in the hope there will be something for all interests and abilities. The estimated times for each walk will vary greatly depending on how long is spent at each landmark and attraction along the way, so please plan with that in mind. Most of the walks are circular but where they are linear I have included suggestions which I hope are the most convenient and environmentally sound ways of reaching the start and finish points.

Please take the routes and maps in this book as a guide only. The terrain in several of the trails is uneven and challenging and should never be undertaken without solid preparation. Mountain safety should be followed rigorously and equipment such as a compass and OS map always packed. Remember that one of the things Wales is best-known for is the rain! Even on the most glorious day, the weather can change at the drop of a hat, so warm and waterproof clothing is essential. Strong walking boots with good ankle support are recommended for all but the town trails; even a short and seemingly unadventurous countryside walk can quickly take a turn into a muddy or uneven section – and that's before we reach the nettles!

I hope you enjoy exploring the fascinating landscape as much as I did whilst researching each trail. Some of the walks I completed alone, others in the engaging company of experts who know their patches like the back of their hands. They certainly made writing this book a much smoother and more pleasurable experience and as such I would like to warmly thank the following people:

Gareth Blunt Photography; David Blunt, Ceri Lloyd, Dean Powell, Brian Davies, Sian Williams, Harri Evans, Ian Woolston, Gary Durbin, Alyson Tippings, Eifion Lloyd-Davies, Katie Gates, Phil Hughes, Tom Maloney, Lynne Richards, Jim Cowan, Sian Parry-Jones, Rhondda Cynon Taf County Borough Council, Merthyr Tydfil County Borough Council, Blaenau Gwent County Borough Council, Torfaen County Borough Council, Newport City Council, Cardiff Council, www.visitcardiff.com, Blaenavon World Heritage Site, Cadw and Sustrans.

Rebecca Lees
May 2012

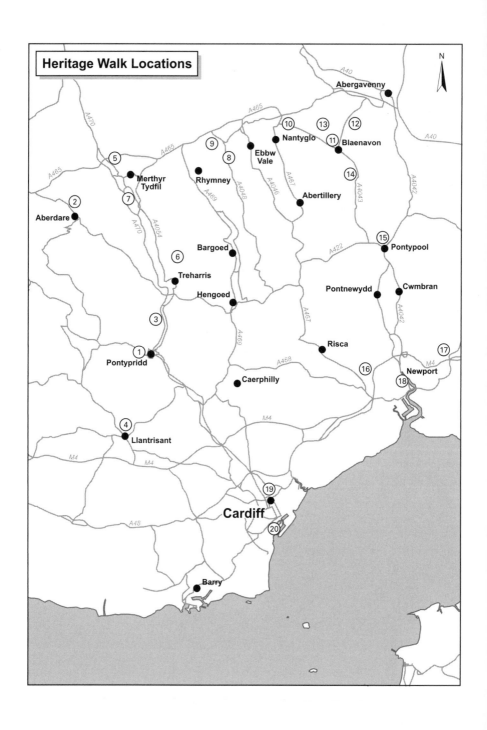

Heritage Walk Locations

N

Abergavenny

Nantyglo

Blaenavon

Ebbw
Vale

Merthyr
Tydfil

Rhymney

Abertillery

Aberdare

Bargoed

Pontypool

Treharris

Pontnewydd

Cwmbran

Hengoed

Risca

Pontypridd

Newport

Caerphilly

Llantrisant

Cardiff

Barry

Contents

Miner's lamp at Rhondda Heritage Park
Gareth Blunt Photography

1. The Tramroad Walk, Barry Sidings

Approximate distance	3 miles
Approximate time	1½ hours
Starting point	Sardis Road, Pontypridd
Grading	A gentle, mainly flat route along tarmac and woodland paths

Of all the images synonymous with Wales, perhaps the most enduring is coal. Wales built a world-wide reputation on the coal rush of the 19th century and at the heart of this reputation was the Rhondda, a cleft of valleys in what is now known as Rhondda Cynon Taf. Whilst the image of the coal-streaked miner is perhaps something of a tired cliché these days, there is no doubt that the industry's legacy still permeates through the Rhondda Fawr and Rhondda Fach valleys and, in fact, the whole borough.

At the convergence of these valleys is Rhondda Heritage Park, a lively attraction detailing the arrival of the collieries and their impact on local communities. Leading directly to the Heritage Park is the Tramroad Trail, a short but pretty trail through Barry Sidings Country Park, which is in itself one of Rhondda Cynon Taf's treasures. This tranquil park is a firm favourite with local families and tourists; the perfect getaway for picnics and rambles. With fishing lakes and a newly refurbished play park, it's accessible whilst secluded and peaceful. Yet many visitors don't realise its significance as the site of an historic tramroad pivotal to the Rhondda's first mines.

The trail starts at Pontypridd rugby club on Sardis Road, which is close to the town's train station and directly opposite a large car park for those travelling by car. Take the path to the left of the clubhouse, winding up through the trees to Woodland Terrace above. Turn right and follow the road as it bears around to the right. Just past the curve, a gap in the terraced houses neatly frames the Pontypridd skyline, the spire of St Catherine's Church at the centre. On the other side of the road the trail is

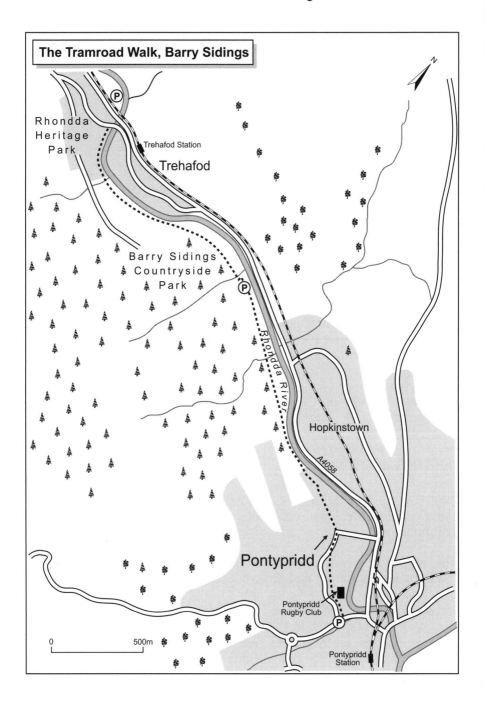

The Tramroad Walk, Barry Sidings

Rhondda Heritage Park

Trehafod Station

Trehafod

Barry Sidings Countryside Park

Rhondda River

Hopkinstown

A4058

Pontypridd

Pontypridd Rugby Club

Pontypridd Station

0   500m

waymarked by a blue sign to Porth and Rhondda Heritage Park (Valleys Cycle Network 881). Follow Golygfa'r Eglwys for a short distance until the street ends and the trail enters Barry Sidings Country Park.

The name is interesting given that Barry is, in fact, a coastal town more than 20 miles away. But Trehafod's links with Barry were vital to the expansion of south Wales' coal exports. By 1880, Cardiff Docks were too small to cope with the millions of tons of coal being transported from the Rhondda and shipped all over the world. A new railway was built and Barry Docks opened in 1889. Eventually three docks opened in Barry to cope with the influx of Rhondda coal, which was assembled at Barry Sidings on coal drams. In south Wales tramroads were, and often still are, called 'dramroads', due to the mutation in the Welsh language of the letter 't' to a 'd', and this trail is often still referred to as the dramroad.

For about a mile the tarmac path runs through the woodland before widening as the trees thin out alongside a pretty pond. This section of the trail is popular with cyclists and horse riders alike. Shortly beyond the pond is a long car park, which the trail passes through and runs alongside a grassy area to the park's visitor

The visitor centre at Barry Sidings Country Park
Photo by Gareth Blunt Photography

centre. The centre is small, with outdated toilets and a cafe that opens only in high season, but comprehensive interpretation boards placing the park in its historic context make it well worth popping into.

The site of the Rhondda's very first mining village was on the riverbank below the present country park. Richard Griffiths, a leading investor in the Glamorganshire Canal Company, was one of the first people to appreciate the valley's mining potential and in 1809 he built a two-mile dramroad linking the valleys' early mines to the canal. Griffiths leased the minerals under the mountain to Jeremiah Homfray, a rich ironmaster with works in Merthyr and Aberdare. Homfray built a bridge in 1830 to carry coal from the Hafod Fawr level to the dramroad, as well as building 16 workers' houses, workshops for a blacksmith and a carpenter and a grand home called Cwm Rhondda House for himself.

Beyond the visitor centre, the Tramroad Trail continues past the fishing lakes and a children's play area before narrowing and disappearing back into woodland. Now just a slender footpath, it runs at a slight gradient along mountainside banks of ferns for about a quarter of a mile, until reaching the far perimeter of the country park at the small village of Trehafod. Bear right at the well-kept bungalow into Cadwgan Terrace, where the landmark stack of the Heritage Park can be glimpsed between the rooftops. The trail follows the blue signs along Cadwgan Terrace to a pub on the corner called The Bertie, named after one of two shafts at the Lewis Merthyr Colliery, which stood on the site of the present Heritage Park. To the right is the cast iron Lower Eirw Bridge. A bridge has long stood here and the road was widened in 1907, the bridge itself being reconstructed in its current form in 1927. The bridge marks the site of the Eirw Level, which opened in the 1830s as one of the early, small sites where bituminous coal was mined. Cross the main road and follow the path on the left hand side of the river. Take the immediate left hand path before the railway bridge and follow the trail a short distance through the trees to Rhondda Heritage Park.

The Heritage Park's chimney dominates the lower Rhondda landscape
Photo by Gareth Blunt Photography

One of Rhondda Cynon Taf's main draws, the Heritage Park is an excellent starting point in understanding the history and culture of the Rhondda valleys. In 1800 the population of the Upper Rhondda Valley stood at just

200 and by the 1850s the area was still largely rural. But by 1884 the Rhondda was producing more coal than any other valley in south Wales and in 1914 there were more than 50 large mines here, many employing more than 1,000 men. The reason was steam coal, which burns especially well. Such was global demand in this age of steam that three quarters of Rhondda production was exported. But this highly valued commodity came at a price and the Heritage Park's sobering accounts of mining disasters and underground conditions deftly illustrate coal's all-consuming reality.

The park centres around a cobbled courtyard chock-a-bloc with relics, including a salvaged steam engine, coal drams and assorted heaps of discarded railway track. The clankings and grindings of life in the belly of the pit can be experienced on a Black Gold Tour, while visitors can also meander along a reconstructed shopping street with its grand 'emporium', the height of retail fashion at the turn of the century. There is a short heritage trail within the park and a nice summary of the Lewis Merthyr Colliery, whose two shafts, Bertie and Trefor, were named after

An old coal dram at the Heritage Park
Photo by Gareth Blunt Photography

the sons of colliery owner William Thomas Lewis, later Lord Merthyr. The shafts were both 1430ft deep and had 26 miles of tunnel – the equivalent of the journey from here to Cardiff and back! The Heritage Park also has a lovely outdoor play area called the Energy Zone and Level 1, a glass-fronted upper floor art gallery and cafe.

From the park the trail heads back to Pontypridd the way it came – a round trip of three miles – although another option is to carry on along the public footpath to the valleys' gateway town of Porth and catch a train back to Pontypridd. Note that there is also ample parking within Barry Sidings Country Park and at the Heritage Park should you wish to do the trail in sections or in reverse.

2. Penrhiwllech Trail, Dare Valley Country Park, Aberdare

Approximate distance	4 miles
Approximate time	2 hours
Starting point	Dare Valley Country Park visitor centre
Grading	A horseshoe-shaped trail over steep and uneven terrain

To the north east of the Rhondda lies the Cynon Valley, perhaps lesser known than its renowned neighbour but with an equal claim on history. The valley is dominated by Aberdare, and right on the fringes of the town is Dare Valley Country Park. The Penrhiwllech Trail is the most strenuous of a series of trails within the country park but arguably the most rewarding, with far-reaching views from a crag plateau and the chance to see and hear peregrine falcons in their natural habitat.

While the history of most of the trails in this book stretches back a couple of hundred years, Dare Valley's past trumps this by a long way. A paradigm of a Welsh 'cwm', the U-shaped valley was formed 15,000 years ago during the last Ice Age, cut by a river and deepened by a glacier. Before this south Wales was a hot and swampy dense forest, but the Ice Age saw it transformed into a jagged series of valleys, caused by glaciers moving south from mid Wales. This metamorphosis paved the way for the coal boom many millennia later; the glaciers slicing through the rock beneath them then melting away to leave steep mountains and exposed coal seams in the valley sides. The origins of this coal lie in the carboniferous period about 300m years ago and were caused by decaying plants forming peat layers on the forest floor. When the forest was flooded, sand and mud was washed up on top of the peat. As the water levels receded, the forests grew back, leading to a cycle of flooding and renewal over millions of years and turning thousands of metres of compressed peat into compact layers of coal.

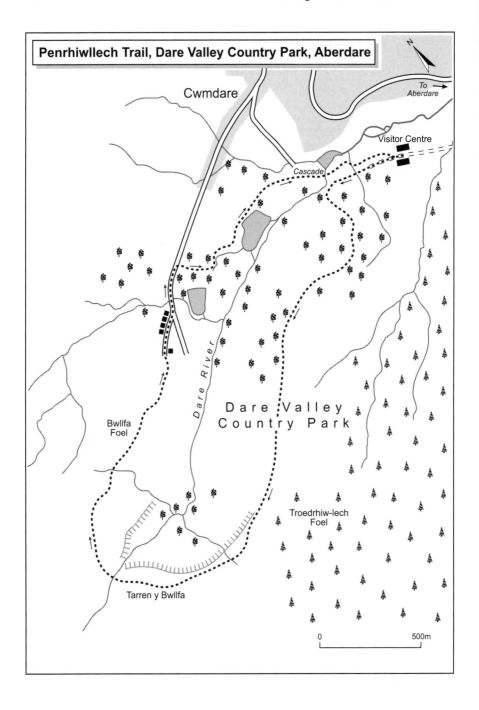

Penrhiwllech Trail, Dare Valley Country Park, Aberdare

Cwmdare

To Aberdare

Visitor Centre

Cascade

Dare River

Dare Valley Country Park

Bwllfa Foel

Troedrhiw-lech Foel

Tarren y Bwllfa

0   500m

At the start of the 19th century, Aberdare was no more than a couple of dozen houses clustered around a tiny church. Then industrialisation arrived in the form of three ironworks and a canal, and by the 1840s Aberdare was leading the way in Wales as a producer of steam coal. The town was dynamic in its output and technology and reigned uncontested for 30 years. But the meteoric rise of Rhondda coal in the last quarter of the 19th century shook Aberdare from the top spot, and the town went on to suffer enormous hardship as the coal industry slumped UK-wide in the interwar years. By 1965, production had almost ceased and in 1976 the last of the Dare Valley's 19 mines closed.

But regeneration arrived in the guise of the country park – the first in Britain to open on largely reclaimed land. Now Dare Valley faces the future whilst proudly showcasing its past, preserving the Twin Tips and an old haulage incline route whilst attracting teams of young visitors to the newly refurbished information centre and cafe. The park offers activities to a mix of ramblers, horse riders, campers and groups, while a rich diversity of wildlife has been attracted to the restored peace of its natural amphitheatre setting.

Starting from the visitor centre, the Penrhiwllech Trail is waymarked by yellow signs and in places runs in tandem with the shorter Bwllfa and Cae

Bwllfa Dare Terrace from the Penrhiwllech Trail

The view from the Penrhiwllech plateau

Mawr trails. From the centre follow the tarmac path gently uphill until you reach a stile on the left, which signals the start of a much steeper climb up a narrow path through the trees. Note that this path is also a bridleway and horses can approach with little warning due to its abruptly winding course. Before long the path opens out onto the side of a horseshoe ridge, from where the first views of Bwllfa Dare Terrace and two sparkling lakes deep in the cwm can be seen. The ridge is refreshingly exposed and one of the attractions of this trail is the landscape's ruggedness.

The path jogs along to Tarren y Bwllfa, an impressive plateau marked by a chunky white milestone, and loops around to the far side of the horseshoe, meeting a cycle path as the descent begins. The path is uneven and much steeper on this flank so extra care is needed. But with the gradient come increasingly dramatic views and the green metal gate is a good point at which to turn back and take in the full impact of the majestic crags. Aptly, it was at this point I heard the distant screech of a bird of prey, giving a further poetic resonance to the amphitheatre setting.

The path drops past banks of ferns and follows a scree slope scraping its way down to a slight fork. Keep to the left and make your way down onto the track leading to the site of the Bwllfa Colliery. Now a clearing at the head of the valley, its former purpose is symbolised by a pit head wheel and a plaque on the spot of the Bwllfa Upcast, a 193m-deep elliptical shaft. Follow the track past Bwllfa Farm and along Bwllfa Dare Terrace, seen earlier from the ridge. At the end of the terrace continue along the road and turn right onto the tarmac lane, looking out for a gap in the line of trees on the left hand side. Rather than crossing the field you now find yourself in, swing immediately right and follow the line of the trees as the Penrhiwllech Trail picks up with the blue and red waymarkers of the Cae Mawr and Bwllfa trails. Skirting the lake, all routes now follow the same tarmac path the short distance back to the centre.

Bwllfa Dare Farm in 1870
Photo Courtesy of Rhondda Cynon Taf County Borough Council

Today the Dare Valley is typical of many sites across south Wales, proudly displaying the worn badges of its past while all around nature is reasserting itself after decades of harsh scarring. Although mining continued here well into the 20th century, the writing was on the wall. By 1910 the coal industry had passed its peak. World War II maintained demand but also took much of the workforce away from Aberdare. Oil burning machinery was being developed, followed by the use of diesel and electric engines. The age of steam was over, and coal was surplus to requirements. But perhaps the dramatic changes to the landscape and their slow return to nature are just another cycle of recession and renewal in the Dare Valley's history.

3. The Taff Trail: Quakers Yard to Nantgarw

Approximate distance	9 miles
Approximate time	4½ hours
Starting point	Quakers Yard train station
Grading	A mainly flat route along tarmac and woodland paths, passing through the heart of Pontypridd

Running from Brecon to Cardiff, the 55-mile Taff Trail is a stunning and accessible route popular with cyclists and walkers alike. A partnership project between several local authorities and sustainable transport organisation Sustrans, the Taff Trail has spectacular views, plenty of waterside picnic spots and a series of centuries-old landmarks.

This nine-mile stretch runs along the eastern border of Rhondda Cynon Taf, following the River Taff gently downhill from Quakers Yard to Nantgarw at the foot of Caerphilly Mountain. For much of the way the trail corresponds with National Cycle Routes 8 and 47 and is well-signposted. As it's a linear walk, a good option is to park at Trefforest Estate train station – although getting back to your car from the trail's end point, Nantgarw China Works, will add another mile onto an already long walk. Also, note that Trefforest Estate is not to be confused with Trefforest, the subsequent station heading north! Trefforest Estate is a minor station and has no allocated parking as such, although there is space on Willowford Road or over the bridge on Trefforest Industrial Estate.

From Trefforest Estate, take the train north to Quakers Yard, named after a group of dissenters who settled in the area in about 1650, a time of great religious unrest. Neighbouring villages such as Treharris and Trelewis also had a strong Quaker influence. Immediately left of the platform entrance is a narrow footpath running along the station's perimeter fence. This leads to a crossing over the track and a faint fork

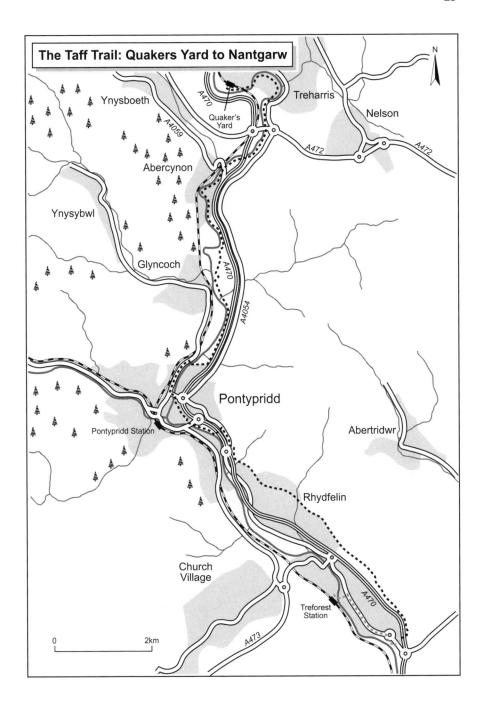

The Taff Trail: Quakers Yard to Nantgarw

A fisherman at Goitre Coed Viaduct, Taff Trail
Photo by Gareth Blunt Photography

in the grass on the other side, where the path diverges. Our trail takes the left-hand path through the ferns, down a number of steps and onto the tarmac Taff Trail.

At this point the river snakes into a vast loop and the trail follows. In this crook Brunel's Goitre Coed Viaduct decisively slices its way through the treetops. Opened in 1841, it carried the Taff Vale Railway from Merthyr to Cardiff. The TVR, primarily a mineral and not a passenger line, eventually became the most profitable railway company in Britain and was essential to the Merthyr iron masters as a means of transporting their goods. The viaduct was widened in 1862, with the addition of another stone bridge embedded next to the original crossing. As the Taff straightens south the trail passes a peaceful chalet park before crossing Goitre Coed Road and continuing along Tram Road Side behind a row of cottages (clearly signposted as the Taff Trail). The route passes under the thundering A472; if you look up you will see the nets lining the carriageway to catch bottles and cans flung out of cars by motorists.

The trail stretches to Abercynon, where it passes the fire station and turns left. As it does so the once-proud Navigation House pub comes into view; this was the headquarters of the Glamorganshire Canal Company and of major significance as a trading link between Merthyr and Cardiff. With the convergence of the Rivers Cynon and Taff, 'the Basin', as this area was known, was the point from which iron from the Dowlais, Penydarren and Plymouth works headed south. Imported iron ore was also sent north from here to Merthyr. The canal had been created along the west side of the River Taff, descending via 16 locks from Cefn Glas to river level, and the Basin would have been a flurry of dockyard activity in its heyday. This is humorously brought to life in Cordell's *Song of the Earth*, which opens with the Evan family sailing in a barge from Merthyr down the Glamorganshire Canal and out to sea, before navigating the south Wales coast to Neath. The Basin provides a quick stop-over, with the proud Welsh gran determined to make a good impression at Abercynon – despite the presence of a tin bath and donkey on board!

The Navigation was also the terminus of the Penydarren tramroad, which witnessed Trevithick's historic steam journey, detailed in The Merthyr Story trail. Cross the road in front of the hotel and walk along Martins Terrace, following the NCR 8 and 47 signs on the right before reaching the end of the street. The countryside opens out and the trail runs serenely along the riverbank, with plenty of benches on which to rest and admire the view. A huddle of rocks below a scenic wooden bridge also makes a perfect picnic spot. Shortly after the bridge, the trail passes the eerie Ciflynydd Treatment Works. The trail now runs very close to the site of the former Albion Colliery, where one of the worst mining disasters in Welsh history occurred. In June 1894, an explosion killed at least 290

The Taff Trail runs through south east Wales
Photo by Gareth Blunt Photography

men and boys – possibly more, although it was difficult to correlate the exact number of men underground at the time. Sixteen men were found alive by rescue teams but only five survived. Coedylan Comprehensive now stands on the site, where there is a memorial to the disaster.

The Taff Trail skirts the Welfare Rugby Ground and reaches a lane. Cross the lane and continue straight ahead until eventually the trail climbs a short bank into Coedpenmaen Road, where Francis Terrace and Lower Taff View are clearly signed. Turn right and follow the road, passing Trallwn Workingmen's Club, then turn right again into Bonvilston Road. At this point the Taff Trail officially continues straight ahead into Ynysangharad War Memorial Park in the heart of Pontypridd, but some of the town's best landmarks warrant a small detour. Turn right, therefore, into The Parade, passing Kenwyn Terrace and following the bend before turning right again onto a short bridge over the Taff. Directly up-river and still visible in the river are the stumps of the old aquaduct leading to the Brown Lenox chainworks. Opened in 1816 beside the Glamorganshire Canal, the works forged the chain for some of Brunel's mightiest ships. These included the *SS Great Eastern* and it was the coils of chain for this which provided the backdrop for the iconic photo of Brunel, hands in pockets and cigar between lips. In the 1960s the *QEII* was the last ship to be made with Pontypridd chain and the factory closed in 2000. After a decade of neglect the site is now being transformed into a £50m retail development.

From the bridge, turn left into Berw Road and towards Pontypridd town centre. Pontypridd flourished at the end of the 18th century with the creation of the Glamorganshire Canal and is still a busy market town serving the Rhondda valleys. Originally called Newbridge, the town's name was changed in 1856 to avoid confusion with Newbridge in Monmouthshire. A number of landmarks are clustered in this top end of 'Ponty', as it is known locally, starting with the Eglwysbach Chapel between Berw Road and the river. This memorial chapel to the Reverend John Evans, who originally came from Eglwysbach in Clwyd, was converted to a doctors' surgery in the 1920s and is still a medical practice today.

From the chapel are the best views of Pontypridd's iconic bridge, built in 1750 by William Edwards. It was his fourth attempt to bridge the river and was possibly the longest single-span bridge in Europe at the time. But its steepness – echoed in Pontygwaith Bridge a few miles upriver – proved problematic for traffic and another bridge was built next to it just a year later! The building on the corner of Berw Road and Bridge Street was the Welsh Tabernacl Chapel, built in 1861 to the design of its minister Edward Roberts and redesigned in 1910 at the height of Pontypridd's prosperity. The pine interior came from Poland and Russia, a result of the international trade generated by the coal industry. Today the chapel houses Pontypridd Museum and Tourist Information Centre, as well as a shop cram-packed with books and leaflet on local history.

Directly in front of the museum, on the corner of Taff Street, regeneration is underway. The unsightly Taff Vale Precinct is being transformed into a waterfront complex as part of an overall £75m project to boost the town, which includes the Brown Lenox development and a multi-million pound refurbishment of the nearby railway station. Claims that the station platform is the longest in the UK are varied, but it certainly had to be lengthy to accommodate the volume of cargo reaching Pontypridd from the Rhondda and the narrowness of the valley did lead to a peculiarity of design, with one platform serving two lines.

From the museum, carry on along Bridge Street and up the steps of the historic bridge rising in front of you. Beyond the Maltsters pub we rejoin the Taff Trail proper as it emerges from Bonvilston Road and follow it into Ynysangharad Park, a beautiful and spacious oasis in the middle of urban Pontypridd. If you have time to spare in the park, take a look at the pretty bandstand, as well as the memorial statue to Evan James and his son James James, who composed the Welsh national anthem *Hen Wlad Fy*

William Edwards' groundbreaking bridge in Pontypridd
Photo by Gareth Blunt Photography

Nhadau (*Land of my Fathers*). The Taff Trail runs along the left-hand perimeter of the park, past the football pitch, and exits via a cheerfully graffiti-d underpass.

A short distance from here, a footpath on the left hand side crosses the busy A470 dual carriageway and joins Pentrebach Road, where a neat row of cottages called Oddfellows Place was the headquarters of a number of early friendly societies. We are now below Pontypridd Common, which has strong links with Dr William Price, detailed further in Walk 4, and has a number of trails of its own. Leaflets on these are available at Pontypridd Museum. From here there are also good views of the sprawling University of Glamorgan campus on the far hillside.

At the end of Pentrebach Road blue cycle signs point towards Cemetery Road on the left. Follow this to the mini-roundabout, with Glyntaf Lower College on the right, and look for the narrow footpath running between the college and the road ahead. Glyntaf is parallel to Trefforest on the opposite hillside, where Francis Crawshay established a major tinplate works. The next two miles constitute an uneventful but peaceful stretch above Rhydyfelin and Upper Boat, with Trefforest Industrial Estate on the valley floor below. Eventually the trail passes under a stone bridge, immediately after which a short path on the right doubles back to the top of the bridge. From here the road curves around to the left and follows Heol y Bwnsi, a narrow country lane running parallel to but above the Taff Trail, downhill to Nantgarw.

At the bottom of Heol y Bwnsi, as the road sweeps to the left, look for the footpath on the right. This takes you across the A470 dual carriageway and towards Tyla Gwyn, where Nantgarw China Works is situated. It was established in 1813 by Derby artist William Billingsley and his son-in-law, Samuel Walker, who bought Ty Nantgarw on the banks of the Glamorganshire Canal to allow them to transport porcelain from Cardiff to London. They produced exceptionally white porcelain which needed to be fired in temperatures of 1,250°C – although the exceptional heat ruined an incredible 90% of production! The pair failed to make the business viable and eventually absconded to Coalport, leaving behind a trove of unfinished pieces. Today Ty Nantgarw is a small but inviting museum and pottery run by the Friends of Nantgarw China Works, with pieces by local ceramicists and craftspeople on sale and talks available by appointment.

The China Works marks the end of the trail proper, although there's still that extra mile for walkers who parked at Trefforest Estate. Cross the roundabout and follow Oxford Road and Main Avenue as far as the Pottery pub and restaurant. Turn left into Powys Road, bear right over the bridge and left up the steps to your starting point in Willowford Road.

4. Llantrisant Town Trail

Approximate distance	2½ miles
Approximate time	1 hour
Starting point	Heol Sarn car park, Llantrisant
Grading	A short town trail including steep streets and a hilltop climb

Much of south east Wales' history is relatively recent, its existence rooted in industrialisation. In contrast stands the ancient hill town of Llantrisant, where a sophisticated Celtic community is thought to have developed about 1,400 years ago. This is a pretty trail around cobbled streets crammed with historic features, as well as a number of modern boutiques, galleries and cafes.

Llantrisant means 'the church of the three saints' and takes its name from the parish church dedicated to Illtyd, Gwynno and Tyfodwg. The town sprawls around the church, which was originally built by the Normans when they arrived at the end of the 11th century, although the tower now dominating the hilltop skyline was a later addition. Llantrisant was strategically important for the Normans as it allowed them to keep an eye on the Welsh tribes to the north whilst commanding fine views over the conquered Vale of Glamorgan. They quickly set about building a stone castle on the site of a wooden fort and continued to improve defences for the next 250-300 years. By early Tudor times the town's importance had declined, although it enjoyed a brief revival in the 19th century when dozens of pubs and shops sprang up within a few streets of each other.

The trail starts on Llantrisant Common, a few yards from the car park at the bottom of Heol y Sarn. Today the common is occupied only by horses and cattle, but a plaque on the cemetery gate commemorates the presence of American airmen here during World War II prior to the Normandy landings. Walk up the hill to the Bull Ring, the name derived from the popular sport of bull baiting using tethered dogs. So large were the crowds at these events that, when the sport was eventually banned in the town in 1827, it was not due to any notion of animal cruelty but because of the unruly behaviour of spectators!

In the centre of the Bull Ring is a statue of Dr William Price, arms outstretched. One of Welsh history's most colourful characters, he was either a visionary or a great eccentric, depending on which way you look at it. Born in Rudry, near Caerphilly, he worked as a surgeon at the Brown Lenox chainworks and Crawshay's tinplate works in Pontypridd before coming to Llantrisant in his 70s. A radical revolutionary, he led the Pontypridd Chartists and was a self-proclaimed druid, but it's for pioneering the legalisation of cremation in Britain that he is best remembered. In 1884 he was tried after cremating the body of his baby son, Iesu Grist (Jesus Christ), but he was found not guilty of committing an offence and the case proved an historic turning point in his campaign

A statue of the flamboyant Dr William Price

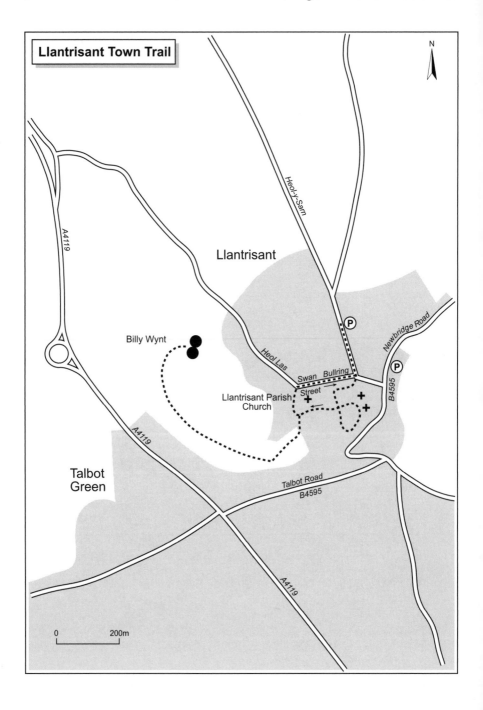

Llantrisant Town Trail

N

Heol-y-Sarn

A4119

Llantrisant

Billy Wynt

Heol Las

P

Newbridge Road

Swan Bullring
Street

P

B4595

Llantrisant Parish
Church

Talbot
Green

A4119

Talbot Road
B4595

A4119

0   200m

to legalise the practice. He was himself cremated at Cae'r-lan Fields near Llantrisant when he died at the age of 92 – after fathering two children with his mistress in his 80s.

Also at the Bull Ring is the Model House, once the Union Workhouse but now used as studios and galleries by local artists and craftspeople. The town pump in front of the building has recently been restored. The trail follows George Street, to the left of the Model House, where a blue plaque marks 'Y Pwysty', or the weighing house. The weight of goods sold at the town's markets and fairs was regulated here, and it was where the town scales were kept. Turn left in front of Y Pwysty to the Guildhall, built in 1773 and used as the hundred court, which was first held in the town sometime after 1246.

We are now on Castle Green, where several layers of Llantrisant's past are preserved within a compact space. In front of the Guildhall are the town stocks, whilst overshadowing both is the crumbling tower of Llantrisant Castle. Like the church, the castle was constructed by the Normans in around 1096 and fortified in stone by the powerful Richard de Clare in 1246. The Middle Ages were ripe with intrigue, double crossing and plot, and the town is reputed to have played a part in the downfall of King Edward II. He was arrested in nearby Tonyrefail by the supporters of his wife Isabella and said to have been imprisoned overnight in Llantrisant before meeting a grisly end in the dungeon of Berkeley Castle.

A path to the left of the castle performs a quick circle around its railings before arriving back on the Green in front of a large slab. This proudly commemorates the 650th anniversary of the granting of the charter to the town and also marks the presence of an army of longbow men from Glamorgan at the Battle of Crecy in 1346. Popular belief is that the charter was given in reward for the heroic efforts at the battle of these highly skilled archers, but in fact it had been bestowed a few months earlier. But Crecy did give Wales the national symbol and motto which are still proudly borne today. In victory the Prince of Wales, known as the Black Prince, took the defeated King of Bohemia's emblem of three white feathers, as was the custom of war, and adopted the motto 'Ich Dien' – I serve.

The charter conferred privileges on the burgesses, or freemen, of the town and created a 'free borough' aimed at protecting trade. An ancient ceremony called the 'beating the bounds' is still held every seven years, usually in July. This seven-mile walk marking the boundaries of the ancient borough is undertaken by the current freemen, who start and finish at a boundary stone known as the Maen Llwyd, where the tradition of ceremoniously 'bumping' the son of a freeman is still observed. Freemanship is passed through families, but only on the male side, allowing the son, son-in-law or grandson to join, but not the daughter. The Freemen's land, which includes Castle Green, the Town Hall, the Graig Mountain and the 360-acre Llantrisant Common, is managed by the Llantrisant Town Trust.

Leave Castle Green by the gate to the right of the castle and cross the street to enter the churchyard. The parish church was built on the site of a pagan place of worship and inside is an inscribed Celtic cross dating back to the seventh century. The massive tower was added in the 15th century and in Victorian times the church underwent a typically

Llantrisant parish church from the south

The 'Billy Wynt' tower above Llantrisant town centre

fashionable Gothic refurbishment, leading to the discovery of a number of Celtic relics.

Follow the path to the left around the south side of the church, which has stunning views towards the Bristol Channel. Turn left out of the gate on the far side of the churchyard into School Street and bear downhill for a short distance. Take the second left then immediately turn right into Heol y Graig, following the terrace of chocolate box cottages until the lane reaches a gate into open countryside. After about 50m take the right hand fork, and from here it's a short but steep haul up the side of the Graig Mountain to Yr Hen Felin Wynt, known locally as Billy Wynt. History has romanticised the stumpy tower as a windmill destroyed in a battle between the Normans and the Welsh, but it's more likely to have been an auxiliary tower to the castle and was probably used in Napoleonic times. In 1893 it was restored as a folly by the Town Trust.

From Billy Wynt, retrace your steps down the hill and along Heol y Graig to the church. Don't go back into the churchyard through the side gate you exited from earlier, but follow the road to the corner of Swan Street, where the churchyard's main gate is situated. On the wall of the terraced houses opposite is a blue plaque commemorating the former Parish Workhouse. This opened in 1784 and was not as brutal as the feared Union Workhouse, which opened some years later. Conditions in the Parish Workhouse were relatively gentle and inhabitants would have been paid out of parish funds.

Follow Swan Street back to the Bull Ring, which is where Llantrisant's galleries and shops are mainly clustered. The diverse boutiques are the antithesis of High Street shopping and although Llantrisant isn't large, it's easy to lose a few hours mooching around at the end of the trail.

5. Castle to Castle, Merthyr Tydfil

Approximate distance	7½ miles
Approximate time	3 hours
Starting point	Cyfarthfa Castle and Park
Grading	An urban and countryside trail with some strenuous climbs and narrow paths

This trail is a round trip through Merthyr Tydfil's industrial, medieval and Roman past. Merthyr was at the core of the industrial revolution but her history goes back much further, so it's fitting that the trail starts at the iconic Cyfarthfa Castle and goes back in time past the ruins of Morlais and along the route of a Roman road.

Cyfarthfa Castle was built at a cost of £30,000 in 1824
Photo courtesy of Merthyr Tydfil County Borough Council

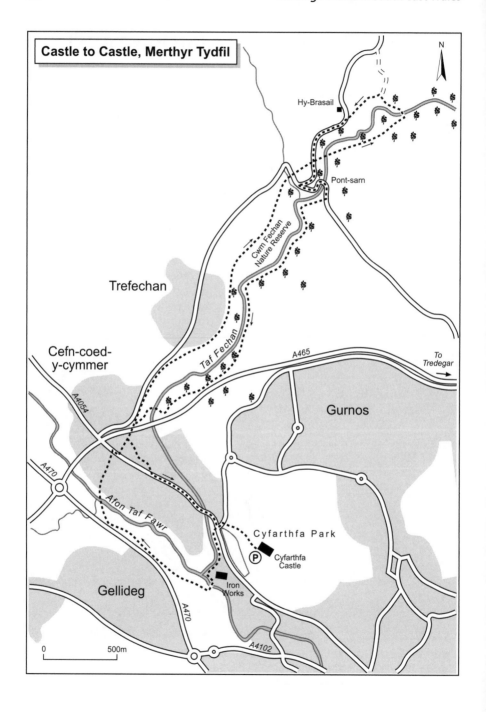

Castle to Castle, Merthyr Tydfil

The name Merthyr Tydfil originates from the fifth century saint Tydfil, the daughter of the Chieftain of Brycheiniog. Legend has it that she died a martyr but 'Merthyr' is more likely to derive from the word 'martyrium', meaning a saint's burial site or church. In Norman times the area was a stronghold of the powerful Gilbert de Clare, the Lord of Glamorgan, who controlled vast swathes of south Wales and the Marches. But it was the age of iron which catapulted Merthyr to centre stage, making her the unofficial capital of Wales with a population more than two and a half times the size of Cardiff's by the 1850s.

Iron founding and coal mining had been practised in Merthyr since Tudor times and there were iron foundries at Pontygwaith, Pontrhun and Blaencannaid in the mid-1700s. But these were very small operations and the area was still very rural in 1723, when the author Daniel Defoe visited the town. Yet a century later Cyfarthfa, under the Crawshays, had became 'the greatest ironworks in the world' due to Richard Crawshay's willingness to adopt new techniques and harness water power from the Glamorganshire Canal. The Crawshay's castle is where the trail starts and ends and although she is now a little frayed around the edges, her dominance is still visible. Cyfarthfa sits elevated above the town, overlooking the site of the vast ironworks which funded it. Built in just 12 months in 1824, the castle was the height of sumptuousness in its day, with its own brewery, dairy and icehouse, as well as huge glasshouses in the grounds for growing exotic fruits.

Facing the castle, follow the drive to the left out of the park at the side gates. Turn left, cross the main road and follow the lane opposite, which leads downhill into a small industrial estate. The established right of way is on the right side of the lane, next to the barrier. Head straight through the estate and exit via Pont y Cafnau, the world's oldest surviving cast-iron bridge. The name means 'bridge of the troughs' and originates from the two water troughs which fed into the nearby ironworks. Commissioned in 1793, Pont y Cafnau was built using traditional timber joints, as newer technology was yet to be developed. Designed by Cyfarthfa Ironworks engineer Watkin George, Pont y Cafnau supported a 606ft-long wooden aqueduct carrying water into the ironworks, which in turn drove a 50ft waterwheel capable of carrying 25 tons of water per minute. This water-powered system was replaced with a steam engine early in the 19th century.

Across the bridge follow the narrow footpath to a wider path. Turn left and walk a short distance until the stony expanse of Cyfarthfa Ironworks unfolds on the right hand side. Cyfarthfa was the largest of four main ironworks in Merthyr and the remains of six of its original seven blast furnaces, rising up from the wasteland, are a formidable reminder of its sheer scale. The furnaces were where metallic iron was made and were considered to be the heart of the works. Standing in the cavernous archway of the ruins it's easy to appreciate the impact this 24/7 operation had on local communities. The works' blazing fires lit up the sky for miles around, making night time as bright as day, and the noise would have been inescapable.

Established in 1765, the works expanded rapidly with the arrival of the Crawshays in the 1780s. By the time of the Napoleonic Wars, Cyfarthfa had carved out a place as a war weapons leader and so important was the works to the success of the Navy that Lord Nelson visited during his tour of Wales and England in 1802. The Crawshays even included a pile of cannonballs in their family crest! Merthyr continued to prosper because of her ability to produce pig iron and, at its peak in 1847, the Cyfarthfa

The Cyfarthfa ironworks was the largest in Merthyr

works employed more than 2,000 men. But Robert Crawshay was reluctant to adapt to the flourishing steel industry and Cyfarthfa closed for a spell. It re-opened as a steelworks in the 1880s under Robert's sons but the site never regained eminence over the more forward-thinking Dowlais and eventually closed in 1919 after a brief revival making World War I ammunition.

Return to the tarmac path and retrace your steps, passing the smaller path back to Pont y Cafnau and continuing onto the magnificent Cefn Coed y Cymmer viaduct. Built in 1866 to carry the Brecon to Merthyr railway over the Taff, it stands at 115ft tall and cost £25,000. With 15 arches, it's a rare example of a curved viaduct, designed this way to circumvent Robert Crawshay's land. From the viaduct you can see most of Merthyr, including in the distance the controversial Ffos y Fran site, one of the largest open cast mines in Europe.

The trail continues over the viaduct and past the picturesque Station Hotel, crossing the T-junction and turning right in front of the Drovers' Arms. Take the next left and follow the brown Taff Trail signs to St John the Baptist Church at the end of the road. To the left of the church is a thin path, which quickly branches out onto a lovely stretch of the Taff Trail which was formerly the route of the Taf Fechan mineral railway. The track runs at a slight gradient until eventually it crosses a small wooden bridge, and just beyond this the bricks of the old Pont Sarn Station platform are visible. Take a detour along the 'platform' and up the short path on the right to an interpretation board in front of the remains of the Pont Sarn pub. In Merthyr's glory days, this station saw more than 20 trains a day and was described by *The Vaynor Handbook* as being 'foremost in the rank of summer resorts'!

Re-joining the Taff Trail, go under the stone bridge and onto the 455-ft long Pontsarn viaduct. Shortly after this is a cluster of green benches on the right. Look opposite these on the left for the narrow track cutting down through the trees to a wooden bridge, taking extra care over this as it's somewhat dilapidated. From here the trail crosses the field and heads upwards, veering to the left towards a stile in front of St Gwynne's Church. More widely known as Vaynor Church, this is the burial place of Robert Crawshay, who sealed his own reputation by decreeing that the epitaph 'God Forgive Me' be inscribed on the great slab of Radyr stone he is buried under. An authoritarian character, Robert insisted that his eldest daughter Rose Harriet never leave Cyfarthfa. When she did eventually marry, Robert reacted spitefully by disinheriting her children, an act he later regretted.

In the far corner of the graveyard, behind the church, is a headstone commissioned by Robert's wife Rose Mary in memory of astronomer Thomas Norbury. Rose Mary was ahead of her time in many ways, advocating women's rights, and was a great philanthropist. She spent more time in London than with her family at Cyfarthfa so it's intriguing that she selected Vaynor for Norbury's memorial. Was this the last laugh at an unhappy marriage? Also buried in the churchyard is Catherine Morgan, who died in 1794 aged 106, having lived through the reigns of seven monarchs!

From the churchyard the trail goes left, but before continuing take a look at the former Church Tavern just in front of the church. It was built on the foundations of a 13th century tithe barn and in the 1700s the local circuit court was held upstairs. Carry on along the track past the ruins of the Norman church, built in 1295 on the spot of an earlier wooden church and now going to sorrowful rack and ruin among the trees. At this point the path starts to wind steeply through the woodland until it plateaus. The crag opposite is the site of Morlais Castle, now reduced to ruined walls and a well-preserved crypt built in 1270. The field between our trail and Morlais is said to be the battlefield of an encounter between the Lord of Glamorgan, Gilbert de Clare, who built Morlais Castle, and Humphrey de Bohun, Lord of Brecknock. The grassy mound is reputedly the burial spot for the dead soldiers, but the less exciting probability is that it was the basis of an earlier motte and bailey castle. The long-running dispute over land between de Clare and de Bohun only stopped when Edward I intervened.

The trail continues from here to the road between Pontsarn and Ponsticill. Before turning left along the road, take a quick peek to the right at Hy Brasail, an Italianate villa built in 1912 – an unexpected sight in a valley of terraced miners' cottages! On the road back towards Merthyr on the left hand side is a ruined building, which was a once popular pub. Just past this a flight of wooden steps takes you back into the woodland and to Pontsarn bridge, spanning the rushing Blue Pool. It's a popular spot with locals, although it's rare to see the water sparkling in its famed cobalt form. Cross the bridge and follow Sanatorium Road, so-named after the

The site of Morlais Castle rising above Pontsarn Viaduct

sanatorium which used to stand on the crest of the hill ahead. This is now the route of the old Roman road, which sliced through south Wales to Brecon.

Turn right into the Cwm Fechan Nature Reserve and go through the small gate to the right of the larger steel gates ahead. The trail now follows the Taf Fechan contributory, and the uninterrupted peace of the next mile or so makes it easy to forget that the busy town centre is so close. Merthyr's ironworks needed coal, limestone and water – all of which were found in abundance here. Nearing the town, the trail passes a leat which was pivotal to the Cyfarthfa works. Cyfarthfa Castle cost £30,000 to build, yet the leat, lake and the feeder works cost three times as much. The leat is undergoing a major refurbishment, and until it re-opens the trail crosses a wooden bridge just ahead of the leat and runs up a hefty series of steps. Turn left onto the tarmac path, which runs back to St John the Baptist Church in Cefn Coed y Cymmer. Turn left along New Church Street, right at the T-junction then left in front of the Rising Sun shop. The trail continues along Whitehorse Court, past the Cenotaph on the left and the Gwynne's Arms pub on the right. Just opposite this is the entrance of the leat, which brings walkers neatly back to Cyfarthfa Park.

The castle is not wholly open to the public but a handful of elegant rooms can be viewed, including a mock Tudor entrance hall and the Round Drawing Room. Cyfarthfa Museum is also here, in a warren of atmospheric basement galleries leading from a very welcoming and charming tearoom.

6. Parc Taf Bargoed, Merthyr Tydfil

Approximate distance	2½ miles
Approximate time	1 hour
Starting point	Taf Bargoed Park Pavilion
Grading	A short, level trail on a tarmac path through a newly regenerated park

Parc Taf Bargoed snuggles in the Taff Bargoed Valley in the south of Merthyr Tydfil County Borough. The borough is among the most socially and economically disadvantaged in Wales but the park is a triumph over these challenges; the result of much hard work to renew the landscape. Whilst the decline of industry has certainly had a cruel impact on

Parc Taf Bargoed is one of Merthyr Tydfil's hidden gems
Photo by Gary Durbin

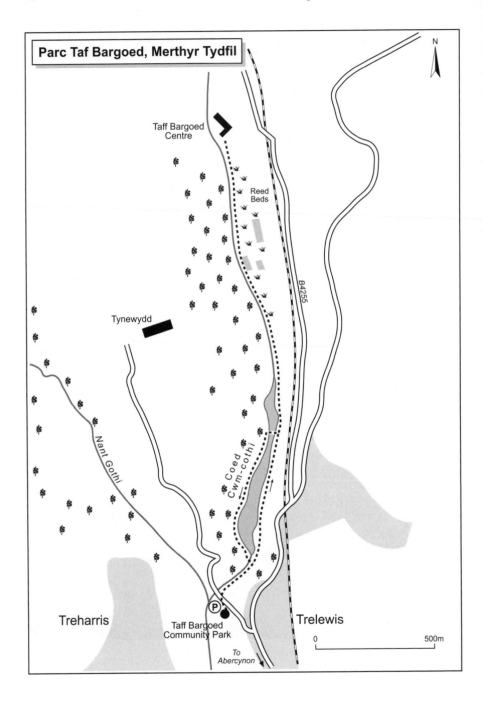

Parc Taf Bargoed, Merthyr Tydfil

Taff Bargoed
Centre

Reed
Beds

B4255

Tynewydd

Nant Gothi

Coed
Cwm-cothi

Treharris

Taff Bargoed
Community Park

Trelewis

To
Abercynon

0   500m

employment and prospects in this part of Wales, this trail has been included as exactly the kind of forward-thinking regeneration needed for the benefit of locals and tourists.

Just 20 years ago the site was the home of three collieries; Taff Merthyr, Trelewis Drift and Deep Navigation. Local people who grew up here say they remember their childhoods in black and white because everything was black; the rivers ran black and clothes came off the washing line black if the wind was blowing the wrong way. The closure of the mines left the landscape scarred, horribly polluted and seemingly destined to become another forgotten casualty of a dead industry. But today, standing on the banks of the park's sparkling lake, breathing in clean air and watching fishermen wait patiently for their catch, this still-recent history is already difficult to picture. Such is the U-turn pulled off by the cohort of partner organisations behind the park that in 2011 it won the Green Flag Award – the only one in the borough. The pavilion is an environment and heritage centre, and has been claimed with a real sense of ownership by local community groups.

The trail starts at the pavilion, an attractive round centre adorned with local art and photos. Encircling the building is a series of giant slate slabs, whilst nearby stand a number of shaft markers, commemorating the site's old function amidst the new. From the pavilion, head across the car park and follow the track towards the lake. This is the line of the old colliery railway, where the coal dram used to frequently come off the rails at a nasty bend! The lake comes quickly into view, its narrow, long form stretching into the distance. The trail runs along the right hand bank, which is lined with wooden fishing platforms and huts used by local canoeing and angling clubs. One of the park's aims is to be accessible for everyone, hence the platforms, and the angling club regularly invites disabled children and adults to 'taster' fishing sessions. The park excels at community inclusion, the wardens running all manner of educational trails and activities such as pond dipping and campfire building, while dedicated volunteers litter pick and maintain natural fencing.

The stretch beyond the huts is one of the best places in the borough to see birds such as kingfishers, mallards, heron and dippers, not to mention otters, toads, newts and insects. The picturesque bridge is a favourite nesting spot for dippers due to the exceptional quality of the water, the reason for which is discovered further along the trail. Near the bridge is

The lakeside huts are used by a number of community groups
Photo by Gary Durbin

a wooden bench overlooking the lake and the park wardens are adamant
that if you sit on the bench long enough, you will spot a kingfisher!
Underwater cameras have been placed in small ponds alongside the lake
and the wardens also claim the resulting footage is just as good as any
nature programme.

A short distance from here, on the site of the former Taff Merthyr
Colliery, the path runs alongside thick reed beds. The beds provide a vital
habitat now scarce in the UK, as the disappearance of traditional skills
such as thatching and basket weaving has resulted in many reed beds
going to wrack and ruin. This has had disastrous consequences for the
species of bird which rely on them, including the reed warbler, sedge
warbler and water rail. But more than this, the reeds are essential as
natural water purifiers, and are the reason the water at Parc Taf Bargoed
is so clean. As part of the redevelopment of the valley, a water treatment
scheme utilising reed beds to filter iron ochre and other impurities from
the water was devised. The scheme, which is one of the largest of its type
in Europe, consists of four large settlement lagoons, 16 reed beds and
100,000 individual plants. Further along the trail are bright orange
lagoons, their colour caused by the iron ochre prevalent in the old flooded
mineshaft nearby. Water is pumped out of the shaft and passed into the

Bright orange mine water is filtered through a system of reed beds
Photo by Gary Durbin

reed bed system, where the plants filter out the remaining iron ochre. The water passes through a series of different reed beds before being returned pure and clean to the Taff Bargoed River, which feeds the lakes.

Just beyond the last orange lagoon the trail reaches a gate leading to the site of the former Trelewis Drift. Opened in the 1950s, it was one of the most productive drifts in south Wales throughout the '60s and '70s. But by 1983 it was running at a loss and, despite a renewed period of prosperity after the miners' strike of '84, it was closed. Today a popular climbing centre stands on the site as another example of regeneration, adventure pursuits and tourism now the focus. Whilst here, take a look at the cheerfully painted water tank on the far side of the site, a relic from past mining days.

Head back through the gate and retrace the path past the lagoons and reed beds. To the right are views of Cwm Cothi ancient woods on the far hillside, home to buzzards and a breeding pair of red kites, which are more commonly found in mid Wales. A number of iron artefacts from the mining industry have been left behind on the hillside and it's easy to picture a string of winding wheels across the ridge. At the bridge, cross to the opposite bank and follow the bridleway rather than returning past the huts on the original side. There is a little island at the end of the lake and at this point the trail becomes the old miners' track. It's a short distance to the pavilion but most visitors will want to spend far longer soaking up this peaceful environment before returning to the start.

7. The Merthyr Story

Approximate distance	12 miles
Approximate time	5 hours
Starting point	Merthyr College car park
Grading	A walk through the countryside and urban Merthyr Tydfil, with some strenuous climbs

This diverse trail starts and ends in Merthyr Tydfil town centre and covers long stretches of the picturesque Taff and Trevithick trails. Today Merthyr is overlooked in favour of the vibrancy of Cardiff to the south and the beauty of Brecon Beacons National Park to the north, yet the depth of its history is surprising. It was the birthplace of one of Wales' best-loved composers and saw the world's first railway steam journey in 1804 – a quarter of a century before George Stephenson's 'Rocket'. Merthyr was also, for a time, the unofficial capital of Wales, with migrants swarming into the town for work in the 19th century. But after the boom came the 'bust', and the collapse of industry is one of the main factors in Merthyr's decline. Today the town's image cloaks her former achievements, which is an enormous shame given that Merthyr's story is just as lively as those of Wales' flourishing cities.

The trail starts at Merthyr College car park, opposite the fire station, and turns left into Dynevor Street. Halfway along is the Court of Requests, now a pub but formerly the debtors' court said to have provided a holding cell in the legendary tale of Dic Penderyn. He was a 23-year-old miner whose name has become synonymous with the Merthyr Rising of 1831, a riot brewed from a bubbling mix of frustration over parliamentary representation and a slump in iron production. On May 30 a large crowd gathered in the town, ransacking houses and shops and attacking the Court of Requests over a number of days. The militia was sent in and a street battle ensued, culminating in the deaths of at least 24 members of the public and injuries to 16 soldiers.

Dic Penderyn, a miner's son whose real name was Richard Lewis, was arrested and charged with stabbing a soldier. He was hanged in Cardiff on August 13, despite evidence of his innocence. His cousin Lewis Lewis, one of the ringleaders, was also sentenced to death but this was commuted to transportation. Penderyn was elevated to working-class martyrdom and the anniversary of his death is still marked in Merthyr, Cardiff and Aberavon, near Port Talbot, where he was buried in St Mary's churchyard. Alexander Cordell's novel *The Fire People* vividly portrays the Rising and starkly highlights the gulf between the workers and the Crawshay family, although in fact William Crawshay was an ardent supporter of parliamentary reform and is thought to have paid for an appeal to the Home Secretary against Penderyn's conviction.

From the Court of Requests the trail continues along Dynevor St and Nantygwenith Street to a busy junction, where it crosses Swansea Road at the traffic lights. A little way along this road to the left is the site of Cyfarthfa Ironworks, outlined fully in the Castle to Castle trail, where from this side there's a good view of the three-faced Pandy Clock. Hand-wound every Sunday morning until the 1960s, when the mechanism was electrified, it's worth a quick detour. But the trail proper follows Swansea Road to the right at a second set of lights then takes the first left into Chapel Row.

This immaculate row of workers' cottages, enhanced at one end by the atmospheric ruins of an octagonal chapel of ease, is a surprising find in modern Merthyr. In front of the cottages is a lovingly preserved section of the Glamorganshire Canal, constructed in the 1790s to carry iron from Merthyr to Cardiff. But the main point of interest is No. 4, the birthplace of musician Joseph Parry, who composed hundreds of hymns and songs, including *Myfanwy*, and a number of operas. Chapel Row's two-up, two-downs were built in 1825 for skilled workers at the Cyfarthfa works, including Joseph's father, Daniel. Although undoubtedly a

Composer Joseph Parry was born in Chapel Row

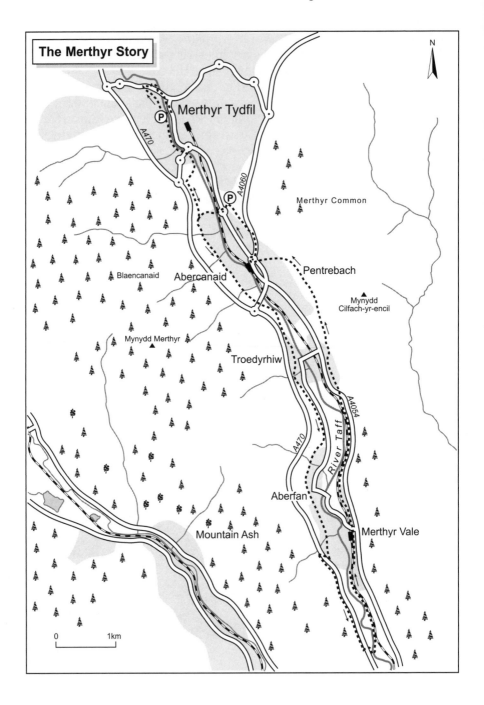

step up from the unskilled workers' housing, conditions in Chapel Row were nevertheless cramped and unsanitary, and it's difficult to imagine the seven-strong Parry family sharing three tiny bedrooms and a parlour. The cottage is open to the public on certain afternoons in the summer and by appointment in the winter, but it's always possible to peek through the windows into the flag-stoned front room and the bedroom in which Parry was born in 1841.

Return to the main road and turn left. Cross at the lights in front of the Wellington pub and turn left along the footpath, passing between the Ty Keir Hardie council offices and the River Taff. This is now part of the Taff Trail and leads back to the college car park. Walk right through the car park to the far end, taking a look on your way at the weir and the salmon pass on your left. The tiny walkway along the edge is for otters! Continue along the tarmac Taff Trail to a fork, where on the right is a nicely-preserved iron bridge which spanned the Glamorganshire Canal. The trail takes the left fork, following the river and passing under a bridge depicting the history of Merthyr in a mural. The path skirts around the back of Rhydycar Leisure Centre and runs under Brunel's once-impressive Rhydycar bridge, its three arches carrying the Vale of Neath railway over the canal. The large house shortly beyond this was originally the lock keeper's cottage, and recently unearthed in the garden stands the arched masonry of a barge tunnel, as well as a number of milestones signifying the distance between each lock.

From here the countryside opens up, the Taff Trail meandering serenely south through Abercanaid down to Troedyrhiw, where it passes the Dynevor Arms pub at Ash Road. Another mile or so along is Aberfan, the name forever linked with the waste tip landslide which crushed Pantglas junior school in 1966. 144 people were killed, including 116 children, bringing the world's press to the village while miners and volunteers searched for survivors. Today Aberfan has an air of dignified peace but the memorial garden and the hillside cemetery, with its rows of glistening white headstones, are kept in pristine remembrance of its past.

The Taff Trail follows National Cycle Route 8, clearly marked by blue signs, to the edge of Aberfan, where it runs behind a redbrick estate and comes to an intersecting path. Turn right and follow the path steeply uphill and under the A470 dual carriageway. The next stretch is a pleasant section in the shade of St Tydfil Forest. After about a mile comes a fork, with the tarmac path bending to the right and a rougher track continuing straight on. Our trail follows neither of these but takes a sharp left down a series of steps and back under the A470 to Pontygwaith.

Pontygwaith translates literally as 'the bridge of works' and an ironworks stood on this historic spot as far back as 1580, when Sussex ironmaster Anthony Morley built a small furnace powered by the nearby ironstone and limestone resources and water from the Taff. During the Civil War the works produced cannonballs for the Royalist army, making it a target for Roundheads fighting for Oliver Cromwell. A bridge has stood at Pontygwaith since medieval times but the defiantly steep humped bridge here today was built in 1811, its style similar to William Edwards' groundbreaking 'New Bridge' further down the Taff in Pontypridd. Across the bridge is the centuries-old Pontygwaith Farm, which opens its beautifully-kept grounds in summertime as part of the National Gardens Scheme. The owners also serve delicious garden teas and give a hearty Welsh 'croeso' to visitors.

The picturesque Pontygwaith Bridge is a popular film location

The trail continues uphill past the farm gates and takes a quick right turn into the woods, clearly signposted by blue markers. A short way ahead the trail merges into the Trevithick Trail, which runs from Merthyr to Abercynon on the line taken by Trevithick's Penydarren steam engine. Richard Trevithick was a Cornishman but his enduring association with Merthyr began when he was commissioned to produce a steam engine for the Penydarren Ironworks. The need for a tram stemmed from simple geography. Penydarren Ironworks was founded in 1784 by Francis Homfray and his sons, the last ironworks of the 'big four' to open. Cyfarthfa, Plymouth and Dowlais works had already taken the best spots, so transport was needed to circumvent their land to Penydarren. Samuel Homfray, Francis's son, sponsored Trevithick's locomotive, betting rival ironmaster Richard Crawshay 1,000 guineas that the tram journey would be made. In February 1804 the Penydarren hauled 10 tons of iron – plus 70 passengers! – along the nine-mile stretch from Merthyr to Abercynon. Homfray won his bet, even though at Abercynon the seven-ton engine broke the cast iron rails and couldn't make the return journey!

At the convergence of the Taff and Trevithick trails, the path runs south to Abercynon and north to Merthyr. We need to head left, towards Merthyr, but before doing so walk a few yards along the south-bound stretch and look for signs of the original stone sleepers laid for Trevithick's groundbreaking journey. Returning north-bound, the trail passes under a tramroad bridge, a piece of engineering reminding us that although now a sleepy nook, Pontygwaith was the Spaghetti Junction of its day, with the Glamorganshire Canal, the River Taff, the Merthyr Tramroad, the Taff Vale Railway and the Rhymney Railway all passing through it.

From here the Trevithick Trail runs gently uphill, parallel to the A4054 Cardiff Road, until it reaches a cream and brown bridge behind Mount Pleasant at the bottom of Merthyr Vale. Cross the bridge and continue along the old tram road to Merthyr Vale train station, bearing straight ahead into Gray's Place. Don't follow the hill to the top but instead drop into Bellevue Terrace on the left hand side, also marked the Tramroad. At the end of the tarmac road the Trevithick Trail and National Cycle Route 477 are signposted ahead. The path continues uphill, getting closer and closer to the A4054 until emerging onto the wide pavement running alongside it. Continue along the pavement for a half a mile or so until you see the black railings on the other side of the road, where the trail disappears back into countryside.

The next section is through Troedyrhiw village, following the blue signs for Route 477 along Lower Mount Pleasant Street to Chapel Street. Parallel to Thomas Jones Square on the left, the tarmac path continues ahead for another stretch before skirting the top of Pentrebach. The trail runs to the new Puddlers Bridge, opened in 2012 and named after the expert refiners of their day. Also at the bridge are steel sculptures of Merthyr-born fashion designer Julien Macdonald, designer Laura Ashley and Richard Trevithick.

Cross Puddlers Bridge and follow the right hand ramp on the other side, not the steps to the left. Follow the A4060 carriageway for a few hundred yards until the blue Route 477 signs pick up once again and point you into the trees on the left. At the fork keep right, uphill, and in a short while, as the route opens up, look for a small opening on the left, where a short flight of steps leads to the trail's final landmark, the Trevithick Tunnel. Entrance is barred by railings but a plaque details Trevithick's momentous journey and it's a suitable place to draw the trail to a close.

The historic Trevithick Tunnel is commemorated with a number of engraved stones
Photo courtesy of Merthyr Tydfil County Borough Council

Follow the tarmac path away from the tunnel and past the Trevithick Stones, 15 intricately inscribed boulders, and to the roundabout on the main road. Cross in front of the car dealership on the corner and continue straight ahead, crossing the bridge over the Taff towards Abercanaid Industrial Estate. Just beyond a smaller roundabout, the Taff Trail picks up again on the right, signs pointing north to the college car park.

8. The Homfray Trail, Tredegar

Approximate distance	6 miles
Approximate time	3 hours
Starting point	Bedwellty House and Park
Grading	A largely urban trail with one strenuous climb and some uneven footpaths

Bedwellty Park is the start and finish point of the Homfray Trail – and it's hard to think of a more fitting subject for the term 'hidden treasure'. This beautiful mansion is tucked modestly into the very heart of Tredegar, the ordinariness of the surrounding streets belying its picture-perfect, surprisingly ample grounds. In 2011 the park was re-opened following a £5 million revamp, and the new storyboards and carefully restored features form a lovely backdrop to the trail.

Bedwellty was the home of the powerful Homfray family, who already owned the Penydarren works in Merthyr Tydfil before getting their grip on the resources in the Sirhowy valley. Until the middle of the 18th century the area was covered in forest, but it became a hub of the iron industry because of its plentiful supply of all the right raw materials. In 1800 Samuel Homfray established Tredegar Ironworks in partnership with Richard Fothergill and Matthew Monkhouse, who already owned the Sirhowy works. Samuel Homfray realised that steam could revolutionise the iron industry and commissioned engineer Richard Trevithick to build a steam engine at Penydarren. His bet that the engine would run paid off when, in 1804, after a journey lasting four hours and five minutes, the engine reached its destination. But the locomotive was ahead of its time and it would be another quarter of a century before steam power was used at Tredegar.

Homfray's mansion, created on the site of a small farmhouse, is a rare example in Wales of the type of great town house more typically found in Bristol or Bath. In 1853 the house became the residence of the works manager, but the running costs were so steep that in 1900 the park was given to the town. It thrived with the additions of public amenities such as a bandstand, swimming pool and the picturesque Long Shelter, and the recent restoration has given these features a new lease, their glossy coats of paint matched by a renewed vitality in the freshly manicured lawns and vibrant flowerbeds.

Also proudly on display in the grounds is the world's largest block of coal, which originally weighed 20 tons and was destined for Great Exhibition of 1851. Cut by master collier John Jones, it was going to be Tredegar's contribution to the great celebration of science, culture and industry in London, but en-route the railway track buckled under its weight! A five-ton piece broke off and the journey was abandoned, the remaining larger block being brought back to Bedwellty. It's now on show alongside a two-ton block hewn from the same coal seam for the Festival of Britain one hundred years later.

The park also has an elegant war memorial, unveiled on 14th December 1924 and later re-dedicated. More than 4,000 men left Tredegar to fight in

The Long Gallery is one of a number of restored features in Bedwellty Park

the Great War, many volunteering in the belief that the war would be preferable to working in the mines. They expected to be home in a matter of months but more than 300 were killed, a devastating loss for a town Tredegar's size. Locals were also to fight in World War II in Burma, where a battle site was named Tredegar Hill in memory of 12 men from the town who died and more who were injured there in 1945.

Exit the park through the main gates (not those by the memorial) onto Morgan Street. Unmistakeable ahead is the Town Clock, built in 1858 from the proceeds of a bazaar organised by Mrs RP Davies, the wife of the works manager. It was designed to be visible from every part of Tredegar so that workers in the Sirhowy and Tredegar ironworks and Ty Trist Colliery would be able to see the time. Tredegar was laid out on a grid pattern and the clock tower dominates The Circle, which was designed at the heart of this plan.

Before the Circle, take the first right. This is Bridge Street, although there are no street signs. Walk downhill past the Siloh Baptist Church and bear left past the Bridge St Industrial Estate, where a dejected board declaring: 'Coal estates for sale' neatly sums up recent history. The trail climbs to the top of Iron Row, with the site of the former Tredegar Ironworks lying below to the right. The land was leased from Lord Morgan of Tredegar Park – hence the town's name – in Newport, and by 1841 more than 2,700 people worked there.

As Iron Row curves into Duke Street look out for the footpath running behind Castle St Church, which takes you through a small car park and to the roundabout near the bus station. On the left hand side of the road is an iron fence bearing the name Tredegar Ironworks Company and on the roadside, at ground level, is a small arched grill. This was the entrance to the level where John Jones cut the Great Exhibition block of coal, although this worthy claim to history is somewhat lost in the blur of cars and buses whizzing past.

Return to the church and turn right into Commercial Street, Tredegar's main shopping street. At the end cross the busy carriageway and continue ahead into Church St, where St George's Church stands in spacious grounds on the right. Completed in 1842, the church was designed to resemble an ironworks engine house! On the other side of the road is a large building dating from 1911, which was the Central Surgery. It was

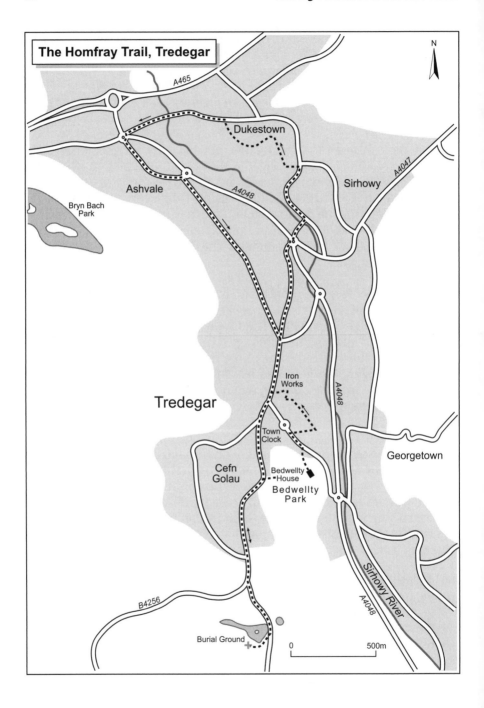

The Homfray Trail, Tredegar

built by the Tredegar Medical Aid Society, which is described further in the Aneurin Bevan Trail and was the inspiration for Bevan's National Health Service.

The trail carries on to the Willows Social Club at the end of Church Street, opposite which is a short path to a busy roundabout junction. Cross straight over the roundabout and follow the road between the Thomas Richards Centre and the fuel station. This road continues over a bridge spanning a narrow stretch of the Sirhowy River, built to carry the tramroad connecting Sirhowy and Tredegar works with Newport. Running alongside the river is Dukestown Rd, where a few yards to the right stand a couple of carved stone markers, one complete and one crumbling. The complete stone signifies Ebbw Vale works taking over Sirhowy in 1818, while the other, from 1797, is all that's left of the original blast furnaces.

Retrace your steps to the bridge and pass through a gap in the terraced houses in front of it into Graham's Yard. Ahead is the imposing bulk of Sirhowy Ironworks, established in 1778 and one of the pioneering sites of its day. The remaining three arches formed part of a coke-fired furnace, one of the first of its kind in south Wales. Initially charcoal was the fuel of choice for making iron but in 1709 the Industrial Revolution was triggered at Coalbrookdale in Shropshire, when iron was smelted with coke. By the mid 18th century the coke-iron industry was slowly replacing charcoal in south Wales, particularly in the heads of the valleys, where blast furnaces could easily be built against hillsides and where there was an abundance of raw materials and water to power the wheels. In 1818 Sirhowy

Sirhowy Ironworks once employed nearly 1,000 people

became associated with the Ebbw Vale works, a partnership which continued until the 1880s, Sirhowy supplying Ebbw Vale with the pig iron it needed to produce wrought iron and later steel. Sirhowy Ironworks is now an unassuming, peaceful spot behind Dukestown Road, where nature has re-established its authority in between and around the stonework. Yet at its height nearly 1,000 workers were employed here and the Sirhowy Tramroad was one of the most important in the area, specially authorised under the Monmouthshire Canal Act.

From the works continue out of Graham's Yard through the narrow lane at the far end, turning right onto Dukestown Rd. The trail is now following the route of a man-made watercourse which originally fed the blast furnace wheel, and the Armoury Stores on the right hand side used to be the Sirhowy Truck Shop, a company shop. After the Armoury Stores, take the first left. The road runs uphill towards a neglected chapel and bears to the right, following Picton Road to a grassy roundabout just before Yellow Row. Turn left into Feeder Bank, the site of the old leat, where below to the left is the Scwrfa. This means 'the scouring' and refers to the early water-powered opencast mining which took place here. At the end of Feeder Bank a very thin and quite overgrown footpath runs to Scwrfa Road, where the trail turns right, then left into St Luke's Road.

Follow the road to Pont y Widw – the Widow's Bridge – where a footpath on the right, signposted Nine Arches and the Tir Morgan Hywel Walk, leads down a short detour between the river and a housing estate. About 100m along the riverbank is a weir dating back to 1796, which sent water along the Sirhowy leat. Return to St Luke's Road and continue to the roundabout which joins with the A4048. Cross the busy carriageway and turn left into Merthyr Road, which leads into Ashvale Road. This takes the trail to a fork between Charles Street on the left and Sycamore Avenue on the right. Both lead back to Tredegar town centre; Charles Street is where Aneurin Bevan was born, although neither his birthplace nor the house he moved to as a boy remain, while Sycamore Avenue follows the line of the old Tredegar Tramroad.

Back in town, follow Commercial Street and turn right into Queen Square. Follow Harcourt Terrace and Park Row to the sharp bend, where the final push up Park Hill to Cefn Golau cholera cemetery begins. It's a steep climb continuing for about half a mile but at the top the trail turns left onto the common and it's all worthwhile. To the right is a large pond, created in

1800 to supply water to the works, and the shallow dam running along the top of it leads to the cemetery. The fact that the graveyards are enclosed sadly within railings only serves to further emphasis their isolation. Disease was unavoidable and outbreaks of cholera occurred in 1832, 1833, 1849 and 1866. Whole families were wiped out in days, and even hours. Cholera victims could not be buried in the local cemetery so Cefn Golau was built, receiving at least 200 bodies. Today a handful of gravestones and fragmented headstone remains are all that's left, but they create a powerful image on an otherwise sparse landscape.

From Cefn Golau head back down Park Hill to the rugby club, the home of Tredegar Ironsides. At the junction with Stable Lane is a gate back into Bedwellty Park. The perfect way to finish the trail is with a spot of tea in the conservatory cafe, which was originally the Orchid House. Orchids became fashionable in the 19th century but were not able to survive the south Wales climate, so the works manager commissioned a special hothouse in which they could be grown. The heating came from a coal or wood furnace in the room next door, a system dating back to Roman times which could be said to be an early version of central heating!

Cefn Golau cholera cemetery occupies a lonely spot above Tredegar

9. Aneurin Bevan Heritage Trail, Tredegar

Approximate distance	1 mile
Approximate time	½ hour
Starting point	Masonic Hall, Morgan Street, Tredegar
Grading	A short town trail including a couple of steep streets

As the birthplace of Aneurin Bevan, the founder of the NHS, Tredegar has played an important role in political history. The town, like many of its

neighbours, has seen a decline in recent decades but several landmark buildings associated with the Ebbw Vale MP still stand. In parts the trail overlaps with the Homfray Trail, and both end at Bedwellty Park, but the ongoing interest in Bevan warrants a trail solely based on his story.

Bevan was born in 1897 at 32 Charles Street, the fourth of 10 children born to nonconformist parents. The family was later able to move along the street to No. 7, a large house which was bought rather than rented due to the exceptional housekeeping skills of Bevan's mother Phoebe. Phoebe's social standing escalated immeas-urably with the move, due to the fact the new house was the only

Aneurin Bevan was born in Tredegar in 1897 Photo courtesy of Blaenau Gwent County Borough Council

one in the area to have a gas oven, with neighbours popping in to bake tarts! Unfortunately neither house remains in Charles Street today, with a residential home now occupying the site of No.32.

In a few short decades before Bevan's birth, the population of the Sirhowy valley had exploded from just 100 to 35,000. But conditions were harsh and the average life expectancy in 1850 was 19, helping to explain the rise of friendly clubs and unions to improve the lives of the working classes. The town was a hub of Labour party activity and, as such, the perfect launch pad for the career of one of the greatest democratic socialists of the 20th century.

The starting point of the trail is Tredegar Masonic Hall, a red brick building in Morgan Street sandwiched between Bedwellty Park – where the walk finishes – and a small car park. The car park was built on the site of the Workmen's Hall, a once-proud building with a library that was central to Bevan's education. There was no trace of academic flair during Bevan's days at Sirhowy Elementary School and at the age of 13 he joined his father David and brother William at Ty Trist Colliery. But during these teenage years he became absorbed in books, reading late into the night after exhausting underground shifts. He was befriended by the librarian, Mr Bowditch, and devoured an eclectic mix of politics, literature and boys' magazines such as *The Magnet* and *The Gem*. At the same time he was soaking up the social inequities around him in Tredegar and this awareness, coupled with his self-education, started to drive some powerful new ideas. The Hall was where the young Bevan and a group of socialist friends formed the Query Club, a discussion club which came to increasingly challenge the influence of the Tredegar Iron and Coal Company.

Opposite the site of the Workmen's Hall is the house lived in by Michael Foot during his time as MP. He won the seat of Ebbw Vale in a by-election after Bevan's death in 1960 and interestingly, a plaque on the wall refers to him chiefly as 'Biographer of Aneurin Bevan' rather than as leader of the Labour Party. From here head up Morgan Street to The Circle, which has Tredegar Town Clock at its heart. On the left is Tredegar Social Club, now in a sorry state but once a grand building where election counts would be announced from the balcony. On the opposite corner, to the right, is the building which used to house the Medical Aid Society. Seen as an early forerunner to the NHS, the Society was started in about 1890 by

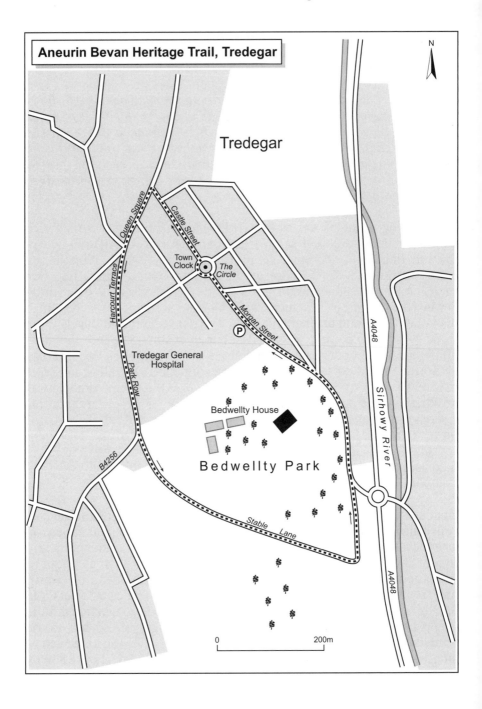

Aneurin Bevan Heritage Trail, Tredegar

Tredegar

Queen Square

Castle Street

Harcourt Terrace

Town Clock

The Circle

Morgan Street

A4048

Park Row

Tredegar General Hospital

Bedwellty House

Sirhowy River

B4256

Bedwellty Park

Stable Lane

A4048

0   200m

Tredegar Town Clock and Social Club in the early 20th century
Photo courtesy of Blaenau Gwent County Borough Council

miners and steelworkers who clubbed together to employ a doctor and an assistant. Most people in the town joined and soon it was able to pay five or six doctors. But it was also scrutinised by the Query Club as it was one of the situations heavily influenced by the Tredegar Iron and Coal Company, with prominent positions going to Company nominees.

Walk around The Circle and up Castle Street until you reach Barclays Bank. Turn left to Queen Square, a neat stone-fronted terrace originally built as a workhouse and school in the 1820s. Phoebe and her daughter Arianwen – perhaps the sister closest to Aneurin – lived here, with Bevan also using the house as a base when he visited Tredegar for his constituency work. The trail runs along Harcourt Terrace and Park Row, where Tredegar General Hospital includes an extension called the Aneurin Bevan Medical Centre.

At the corner of Park Row, before it turns steeply uphill, bear left into Stable Lane, which runs along the uppermost wall of Bedwellty Park. Tredegar Comprehensive School is at the bottom of the lane and it was near this site that Bevan worked in Ty Trist Colliery. The name translates as 'House of Sadness' – an apt tag for a place full of miners who were up at 4.30am and in winter wouldn't see daylight, existing underground and running the daily risk of explosion, flooding and runaway trams. But the mine was another formative force for the young Bevan. A bitter year-long strike in 1910-11 across the South Wales coalfield had ended in the defeat of the workers by their leaders, while 1912 saw one million miners nationwide strike for six weeks for a minimum wage. Bevan's socialism was forged in miners' lodge meetings and he became a trade union activist, emerging in as one of the leaders of the later miners' strike of 1926.

Bearing around to the left, the trail passes a complex of new-build apartments. This area was the site of the omnipotent Tredegar Iron and Coal Company, which owned seven collieries, much land and many houses in the town. A short distance along, enter Bedwellty Park and follow the path to Bedwellty House, where Bevan launched his political career as an Urban District councillor in 1922.

The Grade II-listed house and grounds were falling into a state of ruin at the turn of the millennium but were saved with a £5m refurbishment and

Bedwellty House was a platform for Bevan's political career

re-opened in 2011. The park is central to Tredegar's identity, not only for its origins as the home of the Homfray ironmasters but as the platform for Bevan's career, so the sense of community pride in its restoration is obvious. Bedwellty housed the Tredegar Urban District Council and today the council chamber is open to the public, its curved rows of lovingly carved seats complementing the elegant proportions of the room. A film also plays on a loop, telling the story of Bevan from his childhood in class-ridden Tredegar to his appointment to Minister for Health following Labour's landslide victory in 1945. Visitors can also use the interactive displays and dress up as characters from the past in the Miners' Room, which was used as a food distribution centre during the miners' strike of 1984 following the National Coal Board's decision to close 20 pits.

However fashionable it is to criticise the NHS today, it's undoubtedly a bedrock for millions of people in the UK, accessible and largely free. The fact that its origins are rooted in this small, industrial valleys' town is easy to overlook, such is the juggernaut it has become, yet without the inequities heaped on Tredegar's people its principles would not have become necessary. When Nye Bevan died in 1960 after a long illness, such was public affection for him that a memorial service was held in Westminster Abbey. That affection continues today in this corner of Wales, as does his legacy.

The Aneurin Bevan Heritage Trail can be extended by driving from Bedwellty Park to the Aneurin Bevan Memorial Stones on the Beaufort Road (A4047). The stones were erected to mark the spot where Bevan used to give open-air speeches; the centre stone represents him while the others point to Ebbw Vale, Rhymney and Tredegar, the three areas of his constituency.

10. Brynmawr to Nantyglo Roundhouses

Approximate distance	3 miles
Approximate time	1½ hours
Starting point	Market Square, Brynmawr
Grading	A mainly level walk through Brynmawr town centre to the edge of the countryside

This is a short town trail showing the fortunes of Brynmawr from industrial times to the 20th century. The growth of Brynmawr and Nantyglo was powered by the Bailey brothers, Crawshay and Joseph, who followed their uncle Richard Crawshay, of Merthyr, into South Wales iron. The trail leads to the Bailey family's roundhouses, a pair of fortified towers not quite matched by other landmarks in this part of Wales. The same could be said of a nearby relic built as part of the Brynmawr Rubber Factory, the vision of Lord Forrester to boost employment after the Great Depression but ultimately a white elephant, albeit an architecturally impressive one.

Brynmawr is situated at the eastern head of a series of narrow coalfields valleys, and this strong position led to its rapid growth in the 19th century. The walk starts at Market Square, where the Victorian market hall – now a cinema – is at the heart of the town. From the car park at the rear of the hall, face the Gwesty Bach pub and turn right past the library. Follow Market Square past the hall and war memorial until the Square meets Blaina Road. Cross at the busy roundabout and keep going straight ahead, with the Asda supermarket on the right hand side on the opposite side of the road. The trail turns left into Barley Field Road, which leads to Limestone Road at the far end. Limestone Road was one of the branches of Crawshay Bailey's Llangattock Tramroad, which transported the limestone from the quarries to his Nantyglo works via Market Square. Bailey became of the richest landowners in Wales, an ironmaster with the foresight to buy up large areas of coal-rich land. He also developed a railway and was elected MP five times in succession, although he was not a popular employer.

The trail follows Limestone Road past Bethlehem Houses on the left and turns right at the T-junction into Cwm Crachen. At the end of this short street, turn left as Chapel Road merges into New Road, following the brown heritage sign. Cross the road and immediately take the right hand turning downhill, then quickly bear left into Market Road. The town's markets were held along this wide road from the 1830s. It was also the site of the Bush Inn, now demolished, where the workers would gather to wait for their wages. The inns were owned by the ironmasters and, by the time Bailey's agent arrived – deliberately late – to pay them, they had already run up a hefty slate. Bailey gets more than one mention in Cordell's *Rape of the Fair Country*, which outlines his practice of minting his own coins, which could only be used in the Company shop and beer-houses. The shop is a little further along Market Road, its white, square bulk today still imposing from this approach, although from the front it looks as welcoming as any well-kept home.

Continue to the sweeping bend to the right, where on the corner stands the old Casting House. This was built in front of the furnace; casting houses were always built in the crook of a hill to allow the iron to be

Nantyglo and Blaina Ironworks was ruled by Crawshay Bailey
Image courtesy of Blaenau Gwent County Borough Council

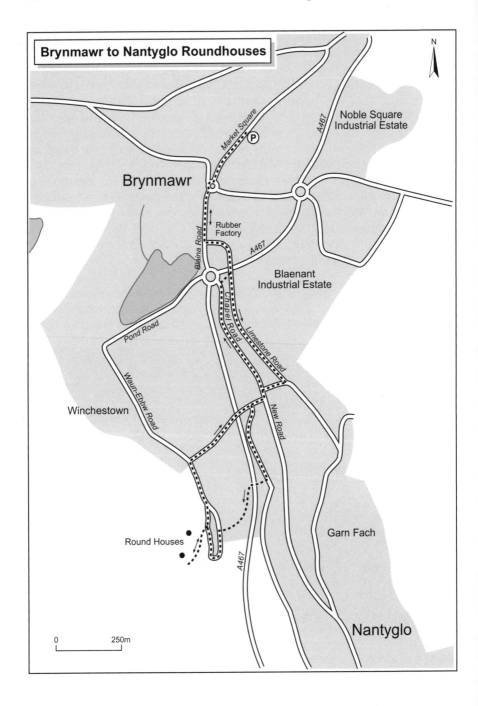

tipped into the furnace from above before being taken into the house to be cast. The building later became a sister chapel for the main chapel in Brynmawr and a Sunday School sign is still visible in the apex of its whitewashed walls.

On the bend of the road is Ty Meddyg – the Doctor's House. Although history has painted Crawshay Bailey quite black, he did fund medical services for his workers and employed a works' surgeon called Abraham Rowlands. Ty Meddyg has been converted into flats but the exterior is still impressive, as befits a man of the doctor's standing, and on the lawn is a sundial cast at the Nantyglo works. Ty Meddyg marks the start of Farm Road, where further along was the entrance to the ironworks and which in Bailey's time would have included a toll gate, as a toll had to be paid to transport limestone and other materials across private land.

Don't continue along Farm Road but instead retrace your steps back into Market Road a short distance and cross the green bridge on the left into the Roundhouse Close estate. Follow the path until it exits the estate through a small green edged with chunks of limestone. Bearing left, the trail passes a terrace of large cottages on the right. These homes were originally the stable block of Ty Mawr and were to the back of the mansion, a sweeping drive bringing the horse and carriage to the front porch. A woodland track veering off to the left opposite the cottages traces the course of this drive.

Follow it around the left side of Ty Mawr's foundations, which still show signs of the original room layout. At the front the veranda base is evident, with the plinth of one of six iron columns – cast at the works – supporting the grand porch. There are also signs here of several kerbstones used to guide carriages along the porch. A central arched doorway led into the entrance hall, which had an ornate marble staircase. To the rear, the foundations show a pattern of three large cellars complete with stairs to the courtyard and kitchen, while behind these you can make out the traces of an annexe and Trosnant House, which pre-dated Ty Mawr and was used as the servants' quarters. Ty Mawr was built by Joseph Bailey who, like his brother, was also an MP. He later moved to an estate in Glanusk, where his descendent Shân Legge-Bourke, the Lord Lieutenant of Powys, lives today.

The Ty Mawr site has been extensively excavated and we know it was set in large gardens, complete with a tree-lined avenue and its own mountain

Ty Mawr was a fine mansion with commanding views
Image courtesy of Blaenau Gwent County Borough Council

stream. Even though it's now reduced to a chessboard of stone foundations, it was clearly a sumptuous mansion underlining the Baileys' wealth and prestige. Its tranquil hillside setting is enchanting and it's easy to picture richly-dressed family members stepping out of the porch into their awaiting carriage. Away to the left, across the valley, is Bailey's Row, built by Crawshay Bailey for his workers. Legend has it that no windows were installed in the walls facing Ty Mawr as Bailey didn't want the workers looking onto his opulence. Ty Mawr was inhabited until 1885 but then fell into disuse and was demolished during World War II.

The trail returns to the stable cottages and turns left alongside the blue cottage at the end of the row. A thin woodland path winds behind the back garden and gently upwards until all of a sudden the imposing north roundhouse is directly ahead. The roundhouses were constructed in around 1816 amid a climate of fear of a workers' uprising, caused by a slump in iron production and the Baileys' disregard for any attempt to regulate the industry. Riots erupted in 1816 and again in 1822, when an early trade union of Nantyglo workers defeated militiamen put in place by the Baileys. The roundhouses are often attributed to Crawshay Bailey but in fact they were commissioned by Joseph. The windows were made from cast iron in case of fire, whilst the inch-thick iron door had musket holes at lower leg level in order to fire at approaching enemies. Although the fortifications were designed to keep the Bailey family safe, refuge here never became necessary and the south tower was lived in by James Wells, private secretary to the Baileys, in the 1840s. The northern tower has been restored and although not open to the public, its presence in this narrow country lane is formidable.

Beyond the north tower is Roundhouse Farm, where the military was stationed a number of times between 1816 and the Chartist uprising in 1839. The south tower is a few hundred yards along the lane to the left. This marked the entrance to a coal level known as the California Level, so-named because the agent, Silvanus Jones, struck a deal with the California Railway Company to provide coal for its steam trains.

From the south tower, retrace your steps past the north tower to the end of the track and bear left at the T-junction. Then take the next right, following the signs to Roundhouse Close but bypassing the entrance to the estate and continuing downhill across Wesley Bridge, which once overlooked the ironworks. The trail has completed a circle and now passes Market Road on the right. Follow the road to the junction with Chapel Road and turn left, passing the English Nantyglo Wesley Methodist Church on the left and the Welsh church on the other side of the road to the right. Cross Chapel Road and follow it past the enormous limestone boulder standing on the green. At the end of the row of terraces, a footpath on the right leads back into Limestone Road and then Barley Field Row.

The trail now heads back towards Brynmawr the way it came. Instead of walking straight into the town centre, however, take a look at the dome-roofed building on the wasteland to the right, opposite Asda. This was the boiler house of the Brynmawr Rubber Factory, which was built after

The Roundhouses were built to protect the Baileys in case of attack
Photo courtesy of Blaenau Gwent County Borough Council

World War II as a solution for mass unemployment – three quarters of the working population – following the collapse of the coal industry in the 1920s and 1930s. The project was propelled by socialist peer and businessman Jim Forrester and was expected to create 1,000 jobs. But it seemed jinxed from the word go. Construction of the factory was hampered by heavy snow and when it finally opened in July '51, it was at a cost £800,000 – twice the original estimate. With a shortage of large orders, production barely lasted a year and the tenancy was taken over by the Dunlop Semtex Company. The factory enjoyed a brief period of prosperity throughout the 1960s but by the early '80s workers found themselves striking against redundancies and the factory closed for good in 1982. The factory itself stood on the Asda site and is now demolished, but the boiler house is Grade II-listed and stands forlornly on the edge of Brynmawr as a reminder of what might have been.

The trail returns to Market Square, which houses a small but interesting museum and the library, both giving a detailed history of the town and its landmarks.

11. Whistle Stop Trail, Blaenavon

Approximate distance	3 miles
Approximate time	1½ hours
Starting point	Garn Lakes, Blaenavon
Grading	A countryside trail in the heart of the Blaenavon World Heritage Site

This gentle, circular trail runs along the valley floor just outside Blaenavon Heritage Town in the shadow of Coity Mountain. The walk starts at the Garn Lakes local nature reserve a mile or so from the centre of town, but it's well worth making a visit beforehand to the Blaenavon World Heritage

The World Heritage Centre is an excellent starting point for any visit to the town
Photo courtesy of Torfaen County Borough Council

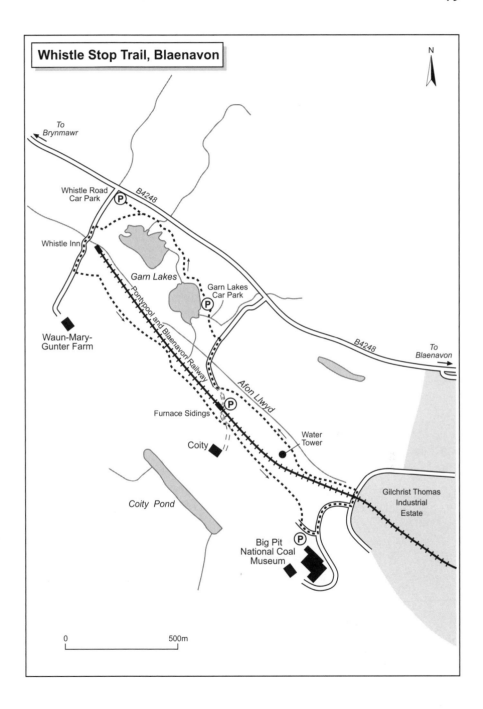

Centre, in order to fully understand the distinctive landscape of this trail and those in Walks 12-14.

The World Heritage Centre has interactive displays telling the story of Blaenavon and its important part in the industrial revolution. It also houses the Tourist Information Centre, which has comprehensive details on the attractions within the UNESCO World Heritage Site, many of which are free and are passed on these trails. The centre also has the Heritage Tea Rooms, which are perfect for planning your route over a cuppa before you set off on your walk or re-fuelling afterwards with a hearty lunch.

There are a number of car parks along the route of the Whistle Stop Trail, all making suitable start and finish points, but I've chosen Garn Lakes as it's perhaps the prettiest spot. Set in reclaimed land, the two lakes and the surrounding area became a nature reserve in 1997, attracting families, walkers, cyclists and picnickers. One lake is now a fishing lake while the other is for conservation, attracting many species of resident and visiting birds such as lapwings, yellow hammers, dippers, skylarks and willow

Garn Lakes are set in the midst of Blaenavon's distinctive landscape

warblers. Above the lakes, the striking landscape of Hill Pits defines Blaenavon, whilst nearby attractions including Big Pit and the Pontypool and Blaenavon Railway cram-pack this trail with a rich sense of heritage.

From the Garn Lakes car park, follow the path to the right, passing the first lake. Don't cross the stream between the two lakes but instead follow the path leading to the right, keeping the stream on your left. The trail runs up to the road and turns left in the direction of Coity Mountain, the setting for many scenes in Cordell's works. Cross the old railway bridge, which today spans the head of the Afon Lwyd river but which originally crossed the London & North Western Railway. Built in the 1860s, the LNWR included the Blaenavon and Brynmawr branch line and was open for the best part of a hundred years.

Over the bridge is the Whistle Inn and a short distance past this, on the left hand side, is a bridleway following the line of a stone-walled track. The bridleway is marked by an iron ladder stile, although this has been rendered somewhat redundant by the ample gap in the wall! As the trail runs south towards Blaenavon, Waun Mary Gunter Farm (Mary Gunter's Moorland Farm) is visible on the right. The Gunters were an important family in Abergavenny during the 17th century, which was a time of great religious upheaval. Mary was persecuted for her Catholic beliefs and this farm confiscated.

A little further along the track are the ruins of Ty Rheinallt. The trail circles the cottage and continues past the picturesque station of the Pontypool and Blaenavon Railway Company, which operates train trips on weekends and bank holidays during the summer. The trains make a pretty picture running along the line, their whirls of steam framed against the mountain, while their whistles can be heard throughout the valley. Near the station is a water tower, which was originally used to fill the steam engines' tanks. This stretch of the trail can be tricky to negotiate after heavy rainfall, as it has a tendency to turn into bog, although it's only brief before the track picks up nicely again.

The route passes the spoil tips, which were formed as the coal was brought to the surface of the mines. Coity Tip was still being used in the early years of the 20th century, although since then nature has reclaimed the land and the tips form a pleasant section of the walk alongside the railway track down to Big Pit. A former colliery which is now the National

Coal Museum, this stands just in front of the spoil tips, its striking red wheel head standing sentry at the entrance.

Resume the trail by walking down the drive to the great wheel at the roadside and turning left onto the road. Walk under the railway bridge and turn left again before getting as far as the large red brick unit on Gilchrist Thomas Industrial Estate. The trail now returns towards Garn Lakes, following the cycle path on the other side of the railway and bearing right just beyond the station before turning left again towards the car park.

For more information on the Blaenavon World Heritage Site visit www.visitblaenavon.co.uk, or call the Tourist Information Centre on 01495 742333.

Big Pit

National Coal Museum is a gripping place and a worthy detour from the trail. It won the international Gulbenkian Prize in 2005 for museum of the year, an accolade much deserved for the sobering insight it gives into the harsh working and family life of the Welsh miner. Mines were in existence in Blaenavon more than 200 years ago but in the 1880s this site really came into its own with the amalgamation of a number of pits. One of the larger pits, Kearsley's, was renamed Big Pit after being widened to 5.5m and deepened and, at its height, more than 1,300 people worked here, family members following fathers and grandfathers underground. Producing a quarter of a million tons of coal each year, Big Pit was nationalised in 1947. But by 1980 its resources had been exhausted and it was reborn as a museum a few years later, being integrated into the National Museums and Galleries of Wales in 2001.

The miners' way of life is well-preserved, from the heavy winding wheels and shaft machinery essential to their work to the buildings aimed at social reform, including a medical centre and the Pithead Baths. This opened in 1939 and eliminated the back-breaking domestic routine of filling tin baths with boiling water, performed by an unpaid army of wives and mothers at home. Big Pit is good at incorporating the roles of women and children into this male-dominated history and in showing the impact the industry had on the whole community.

12. Iron Mountain Trail Part I, Blaenavon

Approximate distance	7 miles
Approximate time	4 hours
Starting point	Keepers Pond, Blaenavon
Grading	A hike through stunning scenery with some strenuous climbs

Keepers Pond with Sugarloaf Mountain just visible in the distance

This walk can be done as a single seven-mile trail or, in conjunction with IMT Part II, as part of a 12-mile, figure-of-eight hike. At the centre of the 'eight' is Keeper's Pond, the start and end point for each section and a perfect mountain-top spot encapsulating the rugged beauty of the south Wales landscape. On a clear day the pond glistens cobalt blue, with views beyond to the distinctive Table and Sugar Loaf mountains and, to the far west, the flat-topped twin peaks of Pen y Fan and Corn Du.

IMT Part I performs a loop around the wonderfully-named Blorenge, taking in clear views of Cordell's adopted town Abergavenny before climbing the mountain's steep eastern flank. For much of the way the trail follows the route of an ambitious tramroad carved into a Welsh hillside, created by the aptly-named Thomas Hill. It passes Garn Ddyrys, home of Cordell's heroic Mortymers, and is at the heart of the Blaenavon World Heritage Site.

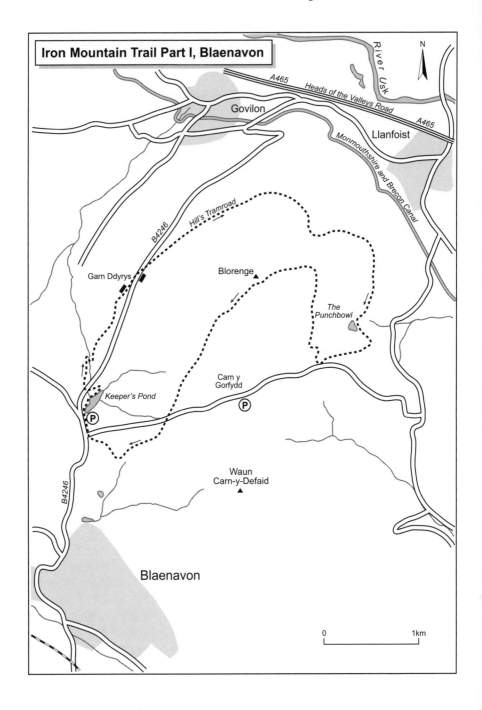

Iron Mountain Trail Part I, Blaenavon

Keepers Pond, at the uppermost edge of the south Wales coalfield, was man-made in 1824 to provide additional water for Garn Ddyrys Forge, which in its heyday produced about 300 tons of wrought iron every week. The once-scarred landscape is now vital for wildlife and, in addition to gaining World Heritage Site status, is a Site of Specific Scientific Interest (SSSI), with former coal pools now rich in dragonfly and nesting birds reclaiming the sheer limestone cliffs.

From the car park, follow the footpath around the outskirts of Keepers Pond to the interpretation board at the far end. From here turn left, crossing a small wooden bridge, and continue down towards the road. The trail crosses the road and bears to the right into the valley of Cwm Ifor. After about 100m the path forks at a grey limestone boulder. The trail follows the right hand path down an old parish road known as Rhiw Ifor, eventually passing a rocky outcrop on the left hand side. Just past here is a junction where the path crosses Hill's Tramroad. Thomas Hill was one of the three industrialists from the Midlands who established the ironworks at Blaenavon. He commissioned the tramroad as a means of connecting the works with the Abergavenny Canal at Llanfoist.

Cross the head of the Cwm Sienkin brook on the right and follow the tramroad gently upwards towards Garn Ddyrys. Within half a mile the trail passes between two long mounds and bears right. As the track starts to climb uphill to the right, don't follow it but stay left, walking between a high bank on the right and a fence on the left. This is the site of the Garn Ddyrys foundry, where the pig iron from Blaenavon was processed by skilled workers called puddlers. Once the iron had become semi-molten in low brick furnaces, it was 'puddled' to allow as much metal as possible to come into contact with air, burning off the carbon that made it brittle and making it more pliable. Impurities were then removed by beating the iron with a steam-driven hammer, before it was taken to the rolling mill to be rolled into bars and rails.

Heading towards two wooden electricity poles, the trail passes to the right of a stone wall and then to the right of the poles. When you reach the road, follow it downhill for a short distance until Hill's Tramroad appears on the right. Follow the tramroad as it runs steadily uphill in the shadow of the Blorenge's bulk. Before long you are walking on the original stone sleepers, now 200 years old and still determinedly evident on the otherwise grassy track. A little way further on from the sleepers is a small 'cut and shut' tunnel low down to the right, now a scheduled ancient monument.

The trail continues around the Blorenge until the gentle curve gives way to a sharper turn to the right and a hollow in the mountain's north face looms. To the right the remains of a building mark the approximate spot of the Winch House. From here the wooden trams were loaded with iron ore, coal, limestone and finished iron and sent down the valley to Llanfoist attached to continuous chains passed around a brake wheel. As the full trams descended under gravity, empty trams or carts lightly filled with goods such a beer from Llanfoist brewery would be hauled back up the hill.

200-year-old stone sleepers are still visible on Hill's Tramroad

The trail continues around the mountain, high above the popular market town of Abergavenny, home of a world-renowned annual food festival. Eventually it comes to a pond called the Punchbowl, which is not a natural feature, the trail running atop a man-made dam holding the water in place. The Iron Mountain Trail now snakes upwards into woodland, where at least one charcoal-burning platform remains from the very early days of iron-making, when the beech timber found here in abundance was used.

At the head of the woodland, the trail goes through a series of gates until reaching a road. Despite the hard work of the climb this is a glorious stretch, with the Blorenge throwing down its challenge ahead and with perfect ridge views to the left. If you wish to return to Keepers Pond from here, just carry on along the road in the direction of the twin masts visible in the distance. To scale the Blorenge, however, take an immediate right at the corner of the walled enclosure and follow the path steeply up the side of the mountain. The path soon veers away from the wall then swings back again, continuing until it meets a sunken track. This part of the climb is a slog, with several false summits luring walkers into a false sense of achievement. The trail passes to the left of a small brick hut formerly used as a wireless station and climbs up towards the now-visible trig point. On this section, lumps of quartz-studded conglomerate stone sparkle underfoot.

The trig point is the true summit of the mountain. To the right of the concrete pillar is a cairn marking the spot of a Bronze Age burial ground. The trig point is an ideal place to rest and take in the far-reaching views across south east Wales before rejoining the path as it heads towards the masts and the Foxhunter car park, named in memory of the Olympic gold medal show-jumping horse. Following the road to the right, the trail either runs back to Keepers Pond via a heather path on the right hand side or joins with IMT Part II by striking into the heather on the left and continuing on to Blaenavon.

13. Iron Mountain Trail Part II, Blaenavon

Approximate distance	5 miles
Approximate time	3 hours
Starting point	Keepers Pond, Blaenavon
Grading	A challenging and diverse trail across open countryside and passing through the heart of Blaenavon

This trail can either be completed as a single trail or in conjunction with the Iron Mountain Trail Part I as a strenuous 12-mile hike. Part rough countryside, part urban ease, this walk has a great deal of variety, including the chance to make a long stop-off at one of the best-preserved ironworks in Europe.

If you have already completed Part I, you will arrive at the bottom of the Llanellen Road after descending from the twin masts at the Foxhunter car park. Alternatively, start at the scenic Keepers Pond car park and bear left along Abergavenny Road, walking along the grass verge until taking the first left turn, which is the Llanellen Road. About 20m from the junction are two large stones on the verge of the heather, flanking a well defined track. Follow this until it rejoins Abergavenny Road beyond the vehicle barrier. Keeping to the left hand verge, follow the road past the drive of Wyndee Kennels on the opposite side. About 10m past this, cross over and follow the grassy track. The trail goes to the right of a pair of wooden electricity poles then bears left between the poles and a hawthorn thicket. On the right is an interesting wall made up from a jumble of stones and Bessemer tuyeres – perforated bricks built into the base of a Bessemer converter. Hot air was blown through them into molten pig iron, converting it to steel by removing the impurities.

This wall made from Bessemer bricks is one of the trail's quirky features

Just before the corner of the 'Bessemer' wall the trail veers to the left, marked by a small copse and a second pair of electricity poles to the right. Follow the path downhill, through the trees, until you reach the car park at Rifle Green. Here some of the earliest mines in Blaenavon were forged, and by the end of the 18th century Rifle Green consisted of small rows of one-up, one-down, back-to-back workers' cottages known as Bunkers Row. The first row of 10 appeared in the early 1790s, around the same time Stack Square was built at Blaenavon Ironworks. Originally tiny, the cottages were extended in the 1860s and eventually each back-to-back merged into one home. They were demolished as recently as 1972.

From Rifle Green, cross the road and drop into Stable Row. Officially the Iron Mountain Trail follows a lane to the side of a cluster of garages in Stable Row and onto land above the ironworks, waymarked to Garn Lakes by a wooden post in front of the garages. But as this stretch, firstly, has become inaccessible and, secondly, bypasses the ironworks itself, it's advisable to instead follow the marker downhill to Blaenavon. At the cottage on the right hand side at the bottom of Stable Row, take the three or four steps onto the green and turn right onto Abergavenny Road.

Directly ahead is Blaenavon Ironworks, now managed by Cadw and with toilet facilities and a small information centre and bookshop. The visitors' entrance is around the corner on Estate Road, opposite a visitors' car park marked by a mammoth seven-ton red steel hammer forged a century ago. The works were founded in 1787 by three Midlands businessmen, Thomas Hill, Thomas Hopkins and Benjamin Pratt, who were looking for fresh, mineral-rich land. Discovering the perfect spot at Blaenavon, they built three blast furnaces and the site quickly established itself as one of the largest ironworks in the world. A row of cottages called Engine Row was built on-site to house the workers; this was later renamed Stack Square due to the great chimney installed in its midst, the base of which is still visible.

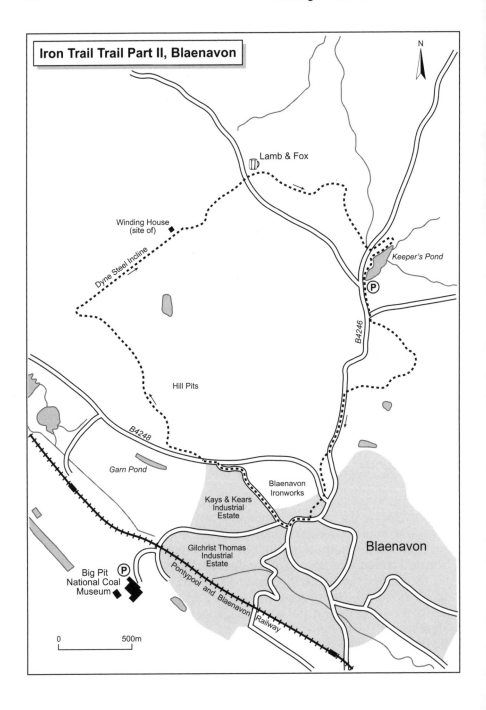

Iron Trail Trail Part II, Blaenavon

N

Lamb & Fox

Winding House
(site of)

Dyne Steel Incline

Keeper's Pond

P

B4246

Hill Pits

B4248

Garn Pond

Blaenavon
Ironworks

Kays & Kears
Industrial
Estate

Blaenavon

Gilchrist Thomas
Industrial
Estate

Big Pit
National Coal
Museum

P

Pontypool and Blaenavon Railway

0   500m

The cottages were recently used in the BBC's *Coal House* series, in which three families were transported back to the 1920s to endure the tough living conditions of an average miner's family. Today the terrace's pristine whitewashed walls are at odds with their former soot-clogged appearance but a quick step inside reveals more of the story. The cottages form a series of mini-museums, with tiny rooms furnished in the sparse style of the 1840s and almost implausibly tight switch-back stairs leading to loft rooms. Storyboards evoke the cramped routine of large working families; initially the terrace housed skilled workers, but by the 1841 census they had moved out of the works and into the town, vacating the cottages for labourers. At the time of the census, an Irish family of nine inhabited one of the four-roomed cottages, adults and children alike employed at the works. The cottages were inhabited for just over 200 years, the last residents leaving in 1971.

Blaenavon Ironworks is one of Europe's best-preserved works
Photo courtesy of Torfaen County Borough Council

The ironworks is also renowned for its role in the production of steel, as it was here, in 1878, that Sidney Gilchrist Thomas and his cousin Percy Gilchrist pioneered a new process that greatly advanced Bessemer steel production. Their technology eliminated the poor quality steel hitherto produced and, within a decade, was being used in ironworks all around the world.

Leaving the ironworks, turn right uphill past the entrance to the Gilchrist Thomas Industrial Estate and follow the road to the T-junction at the top.

Turn left towards the tiny village of Garn-yr-Erw, where the detour rejoins the IMT proper. Walk past the Garn-yr-Erw sign to the bus stop and cross the road onto a track. As this rounds the bend, the trail follows the left fork onto a grassy path and into the territory of the Hill Pits spoil tips. It's a dramatic enough landscape when viewed from the many vantage points across the valley, but up close it becomes almost eerie, crest after crest of now-grassy spoil tip rolling silently into view. The swish of Blaenavon traffic is almost imperceptible and there's a real sense of isolation as the trail follows the rough path ahead.

Soon a well-preserved stone chimney comes into view to the right and the path meets a more clearly defined track. Join it to the right, heading towards the stack, which was the chimney for the pit's steam-powered winding engine. There are lovely views back in the direction we have come, past Hill Pits and across to Coity Mountain. Bear left at the chimney and after about 600m follow the trail right onto the Dyne-Steel Incline. Here the terrain loses the dramatic impact of Hill Pits but retains a desolate grandeur as the incline runs steadily towards its peak.

The dramatic Hill Pits above Blaenavon

The double incline between Blaenavon and Garn Ddyrys was created in the 1850s by Thomas Dyne-Steel, an engineer at the ironworks, as steam replaced a horse-drawn tramroad cutting through the mountain in the form of the Pwll-Du Tunnel. This started its life as a simple level carved into the hillside from which to extract ore, and was extended to create a more direct route for tram cargos. But Dyne-Steel's incline later proved a more cost-effective way of transporting goods and minerals into the town from the Monmouthshire and Brecon Canal, as well as taking pig iron to Garn Ddyrys Forge.

At the peak of the incline is a sense of coming full circle, with the masts on the Blorenge reappearing in the distance to the right. The hike back to the car from here highlights the particular identities of the two halves of the Iron Mountain Trail, Part II majestically bleak in comparison to the lush greenery winding its way around the Blorenge in Part I. The trail plunges downhill, bearing to the right of a square redbrick building which once housed generators, and carries on to the Lamb and Fox pub. This area is Pwll-Du, a once-thriving village boasting two pubs, two chapels, a few bakeries and a school. Crossing the road, follow the path to the right of the pub and go through the kissing gate, continuing in the direction of the masts. A little further on the path becomes quite boggy but is easily accessible thanks to a series of huge stone slabs. The trail skirts a massive rectangular feature that was once a balance pond used to operate trams in a vertical shaft at Pwll-Du Quarry.

Just past this, the trail can be followed left towards a zig-zag path down onto Hill's Tramroad, if you have chosen to do Parts I and II in reverse. To return to Keepers Pond, however, head right for the final stretch uphill.

14. Cwmafon Trail, Blaenavon

Approximate distance	4½ miles
Approximate time	2½ hours
Starting point	Capel Newydd, Llanover Road, Blaenavon
Grading	An energetic walk with some steep climbs and challenging paths

The Cwmafon trail explores the peaceful valley south of the town of Blaenavon. In parts the walk is quite challenging, but across a landscape so prettily untouched by 21st century life that it's unlikely you'll want to go at full speed anyway. The trail crosses woodland and rough, boggy moorland, so good boots are a must.

The starting point is at Capel Newydd, about 1½ miles south of Blaenavon on the Llanover Road. Today Capel Newydd is all verdant countryside and serene views but it was once a hub of religion, with a chapel built here in 1750 to serve as the chapel of ease for Llanofer Church. The chapel is long gone but the site is marked by a memorial cross and open-air services are still occasionally held here. The cross is not easy to see from the car park but quickly comes into view when you take a few steps down the slope ahead – minding the nettles as you go! Returning to the car park and facing the cross, follow the road right, in the direction of Blaenavon, until you get to the corner of the conifer plantation. From here the trail runs downhill, parallel to the edge of the plantation and at a 45° angle with the memorial cross. This section can be quite overgrown and, whilst it's easy to follow by keeping to the fence, the ferns are ankle-deep at a number of points.

Cross a stile in the corner and turn left through the wood, before taking the wooden steps on the right. This brings you to a well-preserved lime kiln, which looks like little more than a pile of stones from above but becomes much clearer if you scramble down the bank and view it from in front. Back on the path, the trail reaches a waymark post but instead of following it downhill, continue across the wood. After passing through a gap in a stone wall, the trail meets another path and joins it to the right, now running downhill. This track is initially wide but quickly thins into a narrow footpath winding through the ferns and bracken until it meets a clear and wide path running north. Turn right onto this, where you will quickly arrive at a small barn on the right hand side. Much of the roof is missing and it's now unused but it lends an air of enchantment to this pretty woodland spot.

From here don't continue along the wide track but look directly opposite the barn for another narrow footpath plunging further down the hillside. There are a lot of nettles on this section so trousers are the sensible option instead of shorts! The trail runs

Torfaen Leisure Route has many signs of the railways' Victorian golden age

down to the A4043, which is not busy but which does need to be crossed carefully as the traffic can be fast-moving. On the other side, go through the gate onto the drive of Glebeland Farm and cross a pretty wooden foot bridge spanning the Afon Lwyd. Follow the river around to the right for a short distance and cross the old fenced railway line, continuing to follow the path to the right. This line was the Eastern Valley section of the Monmouthshire Railway, opened in the mid 19th century to connect Blaenavon and Pontypool with Newport and which replaced an earlier tramroad along this stretch designed by Thomas Dadford.

The trail at first heads towards the farmhouse but then veers just short of it through a gate into a field. It passes through a second gate straight ahead and climbs a steep bank, swinging around to the left. It's an energetic scramble but an interesting one, passing stone railway embankment walls hinting at a past maze of railways and tramways serving a multitude of mineral mines and industrial works. Eventually the

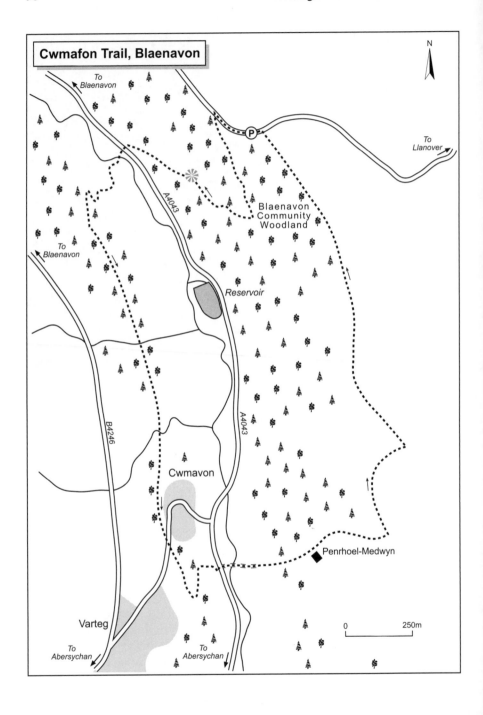

Cwmafon Trail, Blaenavon

trail arrives at a level path running along the top of the bank. This is National Cycle Network Route 492, which forms the Torfaen Leisure Route running the whole length of the borough. It's a lovely path for cyclists and horse-riders as well as walkers and is popular, so it's likely you'll see plenty of other users along this stretch.

Turn left and follow the leisure path for about a mile, passing plenty of features from the golden age of Victorian railway architecture including retaining walls, culverts and bridges. Through the hedges and trees on your left are a number of vantage points, including fine views of Cwmafon Reservoir. Eventually the path reaches two overhead bridges quite close to one another. In between them, on the right, is the raised trace of a former platform, and sitting on the top is a quirky cluster of wooden seats carved into objects including a picnic basket and a treasure chest! It's a lovely feature, adding another dimension of charm to a very pleasant section of the trail. Immediately after the second bridge is a path on the left hand side. Don't follow the horseshoe curve leading over the bridge itself but instead take the right hand fork downhill, along a path known as 'The Snail Creep'. This takes us back to the A4043, where there used

The perfect picnic spot!

to be a pub on the corner which was popular with walkers but which has now closed.

Cross the road and return over the Afon Lwyd, following the lane until it peters out into a path. There is now a steep climb ahead, crossing a track and passing Pistyll Gwyn Farm on the right. The trail goes through a gate and continues on up the concrete road, which is the old Llanover parish road. Near the top of the hill a signpost points left and the trail heads towards the conifers before swinging away to the right. The trail can get quite literally bogged down at this point and is easy to lose, but if you aim for the open countryside above the trees you will soon spot a clearly visible wooden signpost marking a crossroads to the left of the masts. Take the trail running left, parallel with the trees on the left. The path remains muddy but is more defined, tracing the route of a packhorse trail from centuries ago. In the early days of iron production, trains of up to 100 mules, each loaded with cargoes of up to 150kg, would make their way along here on the arduous journey between Blaenavon and Newport.

The remaining stretch of the trail is a pleasant hike across open moorland, in line with the trees on the left. At Llanover Road, turn left and you are almost immediately back at the Capel Newydd car park where we started.

15. The Hanbury Trail, Pontypool

Approximate distance	3 miles
Approximate time	1½ hours
Starting point	St Cadoc's Church, Trevethin, Pontypool
Grading	A countryside trail passing a number of unusual landmarks

The claims of Pontypool, a small town nine miles north of Newport, are often overshadowed by the historic pedigree of Blaenavon and the prettiness of Abergavenny. Yet the town has far more to it than simply being the home of a legendary front row in a rugby-obsessed nation. Pontypool was something of a medieval trailblazer, with an iron industry established as long ago as the 1400s. This was later developed by the influential Hanbury family, who were also pioneers in the manufacture of Pontypool Japanware, a method of varnishing tinplate to achieve a glossy appearance. It was already being used in the Far East but the Hanburys adapted it using local resources and it became very popular in the 18th century.

Many clues to the Hanburys still exist in the town today, particularly in Pontypool Park, the grounds of the family home until the early 20th century. Here a number of incongruous landmarks – such as a shell grotto and a Victorian lodge that could have popped straight out of a Hansel and Gretel book – help make the Hanbury Trail a complete treasure, offering a peek into the indulgences of the rich amidst a backdrop of industrial and rural hardship.

The trail starts at St Cadoc's Church in Trevethin, about a mile from Pontypool. Trevethin is the point where ancient meets modern, its centuries-old church surrounded by clusters of post-World War II social housing. There is nothing in this warren of streets to suggest the proximity of open countryside, yet it opens up almost immediately beyond the church, with the most unexpected views rewarding a short, sharp climb.

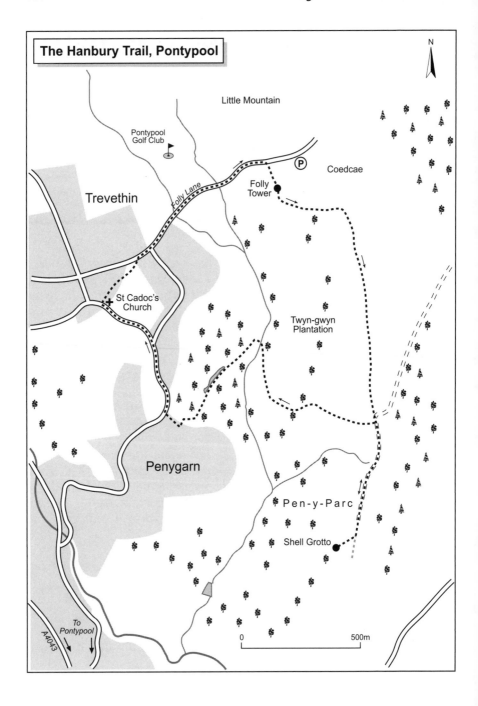

The Hanbury Trail, Pontypool

N

Little Mountain

Pontypool
Golf Club

Coedcae

Folly Lane

P

Folly
Tower

Trevethin

St Cadoc's
Church

Twyn-gwyn
Plantation

Penygarn

Pen-y-Parc

Shell Grotto

To
Pontypool

A4043

0   500m

St Cadoc's is quaint and masterful all at once; charming arched gateways and intricate stonework humbled by a massive square tower. A church stood here in Celtic times and St Cadoc's historic links with the yew tree can be traced back to the Celts' belief in the yew as a symbol of the continuity of life. The church standing today dates to medieval times and underwent a rebuild and extension in the 1800s, when immigrants flooded into Pontypool and the surrounding communities from across the UK and Italy, giving St Cadoc's the largest population in Pontypool. Today the churchyard is managed as a 'living churchyard' to encourage conservation and nature.

The trail turns right into Folly Lane behind St Cadoc's, passing the sprawling Ysgol Gyfun Gwynllyw on the left and then the Nant y Gollen property. The lane becomes very steep but the views quickly start to unfold. At the top of the hill is a green metal gate on the right and beyond this a kissing gate leads into a field, where Folly Tower rises impressively on the ridge ahead. The folly is thought to have been built by John Hanbury about 250 years ago and was renovated by Capel Hanbury Leigh in about 1831. During World War II the Ministry of Defence ordered its demolition lest it became a target for German planes, but it was later

Folly Tower was demolished during World War II and later rebuilt

rebuilt and reopened by the Prince of Wales in 1994. A plaque by the Pontypool branch of the Royal Air Forces Association is embedded in a stone memorial outside.

The tower is open to the public during limited hours at weekends and bank holidays in the summer but even when it's closed, its glorious hilltop setting, with stunning views across the Usk Valley, makes it well worth visiting. To continue with the trail, look for the rough path running south east through the field towards a gate. Through this, follow the grassy path downhill between two fields towards the phone mast. The path soon widens into a track and passes the mast, eventually reaching a gate with a stile. Almost immediately is another gate, then a forked country lane. For now the trail continues straight ahead, although later on it returns to this spot and follows the right-hand turning.

The lane passes the pretty Keepers' Cottage, which is private property, on the right and comes to a stop at farm gate with a kissing gate next to it. Follow the track beyond this a short distance, until on the right you see an old-fashioned metal ladder over the stone wall. This marks a small entrance into Pontypool Park and leads to the Shell Grotto. Harsh railings now hamper the impact of the grotto's features but it's nevertheless an enchanting curiosity where you least expect to find it. Thought also to have been built by John Hanbury, the grotto was refurbished by Capel Hanbury Leigh's wife, Molly, and includes a number of shell-encrusted pillars in keeping with the fashion for shell collecting among wealthy ladies at that time. The grotto was used for family picnics and shooting parties and was even visited by the Prince of Wales, later Edward VII, towards the end of the 19th century. The grotto underwent extensive repairs in the 1990s to restore it to its Victorian glory, thanks to funding from Cadw and a Heritage Lottery Grant, and is now, like Folly Tower, open at certain times in the summer.

The rest of the park is lovely, with well-groomed gardens and family attractions such as a dry ski slope. Molly Hanbury Leigh commissioned the famous landscaper Capability Brown to design the grounds and, during a slump in iron production, the Hanburys paid employees to carry out construction work in the park rather than laying them off. Also in the park is Pontypool Museum, set in a grand Georgian stable block and housing a collection of decorative Japanware made at the Hanbury's ironworks, as well as artefacts from the local glass and steel industries.

From the shell grotto, leave the park and return past the Keepers' Cottage to the fork in the lane. Take the downhill option, now on the left, and walk through Twyn Gwyn Farm. This is a busy working farm so take care not to disrupt the animals. The trail now enters a wooded plantation called the American Gardens, which was again created by the Hanburys. Around a corner walkers suddenly come across Penygarn Lodge, a rustic Victorian cottage sitting enigmatically in the gloom of the woodland, dwarfed by Giant Redwoods and other non-indigenous trees. The path bears left at the cottage and passes a pretty pond and banks of rhododendrons on the right before leaving the park through the gates onto Channel View road. Turn right and follow Channel View and Penygarn Road back to St Cadoc's Church, passing a couple of pretty cottages and Penygarn Community School on the way.

The Victorian lodge in the American Gardens

16. Fourteen Locks Circular Walk

Approximate distance	3 miles
Approximate time	1½ hours
Starting point	Fourteen Locks Visitor Centre, Rogerstone, Newport
Grading	A country and canal-side walk with one very steep climb and some uneven fields to cross

Positioned on the edge of the pretty village of Rogerstone is Fourteen Locks, the start and finishing point for this trail. The visitor centre looks inauspicious enough at first glance, yet just a stone's throw away is one of the most ingenious flights of locks found in the UK. Marking the start of the rolling countryside north of Newport, Fourteen Locks is popular with

The Fourteen Locks visitor centre sits in a peaceful spot

ramblers and dog walkers, as well as with visitors who simply want to enjoy a cup of tea or coffee on the centre's canal-side patio. The Fourteen Locks Circular Walk is well-marked from the centre with yellow and green waymark discs.

Fourteen Locks, like Parc Taf Bargoed in Merthyr Tydfil, is a lovely example of 21st century regeneration. The last boat to be charged a toll made its journey in December 1935 and, in the following decades, the locks became a focal point for rubbish and undergrowth. But a millennium project undertaken by Newport City Council in partnership with the Monmouthshire, Brecon and Abergavenny Canals Trust, with funding from the Heritage Lottery Fund and other bodies, has seen some of the locks restored. Clear of debris, the locks' imposing height and formidable gates give some idea of the scale of effort involved in bringing a boat along the full flight, tons of water rushing in and out as gates opened and closed.

The series of 14 locks, called the Cefn Flight, starts at Lock 21. Made up of five pairs, one triple and one single lock, the series cascades down to Lock Eight next to the M4 – fitting given that the canal was the 'motorway' of its day. Completed in 1799, the flight navigates a drop of 169ft in just half a mile, an enormous feat of engineering by Thomas Dadford Jnr. The end of the 18th century was a blur of canal fever, with more than 200 miles of waterways being carved out in Wales, and Dadford had already worked with his father on sections of the Glamorganshire Canal. The Monmouthshire Canal was commissioned for the primary purpose of transporting coal and iron from the valleys down to Newport, although it also moved goods upstream, including potatoes and wood for pit props! In the early days Newport was the chief coal port in the south, with exports four times larger than those from Cardiff, due to its exemption from coal duty. Two branches of the Monmouthshire Canal were built, the Crumlin arm, which includes the Fourteen Locks, and an 11-mile stretch from Pontnewynydd to Newport.

To see Lock 21, walk across the wooden bridge at the head of the pound – the stretch of water between locks next to the visitor centre – and cross the road. The restoration of this lock was completed in 2005. The signs MCC and MRCC refer to the Monmouthshire Canal Company, which became the Monmouthshire Railway and Canal Company in 1865. The railways were eventually to spell the end of the canals' heyday, with trains able to transport far greater quantities of coal and at vastly greater

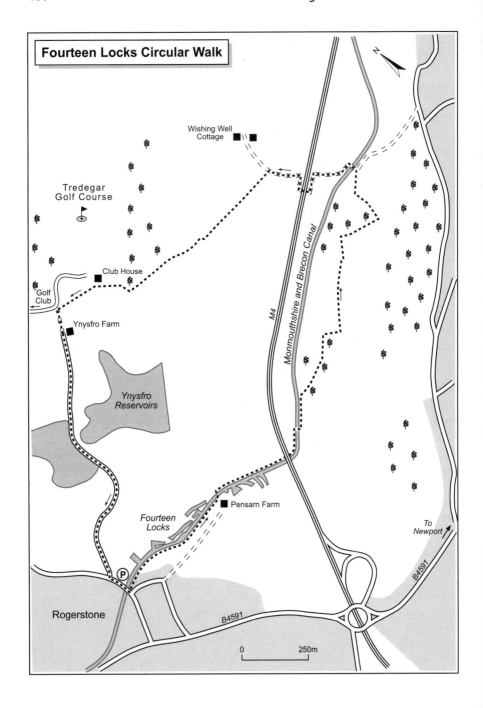

Fourteen Locks Circular Walk

Wishing Well Cottage

Tredegar Golf Course

Club House

Golf Club

Ynysfro Farm

Ynysfro Reservoirs

Monmouthshire and Brecon Canal

M4

Fourteen Locks

Pensarn Farm

To Newport

B4591

Rogerstone

B4591

0   250m

speeds. Cordell's *Song of the Earth* portrays the final days of the David and Goliath battle between water and rail, with bargeman Mostyn Evan and his family being slowly squeezed out of their livelihood on the Neath canal.

Come back across the road and along the towpath to the right of the pound. Locks 20-17 constitute two pairs, which were fully restored in

The restoration project gets underway
Photo by Tom Maloney

2010. Interestingly the lock chamber walls are made from a variety of stone, suggesting that materials were collected from a number of places. The restoration team found a lot of old red sandstone in the chambers of Locks 19 and 20, with rusticated (decorated) stone used on one side of Lock 19. The same sandstone was used to build Newport Castle, the grounds of which the canal passed through, and its use here strongly suggests 'recycling'. It is believed that contractor Walter Waters' budget to build the flight didn't extend as far as buying the stone itself – yet it had to come from somewhere!

Opposite Lock 17 is a bye-wash, into which the excess water swirled as the lock filled up. For years it was used by local people as a 'baby' pool where children learned to swim! As part of the restoration project a dam was built after this lock, which marks the end of the restoration so far. From here the trail continues along the towpath past the pretty Pensarn Cottage, which was a lock-keeper's house. The last keeper of this lock was Jack Brookes, or 'Squire Jack', as he was known locally. Note the outdoor 'ty bach' (toilet) in his garden – the waste used to go straight into the canal! The lock keeper had an allotment and would have been self sufficient, growing vegetables and keeping pigs and chickens.

Cross the canal bridge near the cottage, where on the left is a short fence. Behind this is a lime kiln, where limestone was burnt. The resulting lime

A section of the Cefn Flight has been restored to its former glory

would be used as fertiliser or mixed with sand to make mortar to bind bricks and stones in walls. A little further along is Lock 11, known as the 'mystery lock' as it's wider than the others and has a double shelf but it's not obvious why. Current opinion suggests it was too short for standard-sized boats and it appears to have been built post-1880, after the canal's glory days.

From Lock Eight the trail passes under the M4 and takes the tarmac path on the left, which leads to a stone arched bridge over the canal. Cross to the other side and walk to the gate on the left, following the bridleway sign along a well-defined track. Now for the hard part – a flight of 173 steps climbing steeply through the woodland. It's a challenging stretch but worthwhile for the beautiful views to the north of the Usk Valley from the path at the top of the steps.

Follow the waymarked path to one kissing gate and take a sharp right through another into a pretty meadow. This is a blissfully secluded spot, with a handy bench at the top of the meadow, just to the right of the kissing gate, from which to take in the view. The path then continues downhill to another kissing gate close to a pond. Turn left through here and follow the wide path back to the canal at the Allt-yr-yn Lock. The trail now crosses the canal again and briefly follows the towpath left, before heading right past Grove Farm.

The track leads back under the motorway and to a stile on the left a short distance on. Following the waymark posts, cross a couple of fields and two further stiles. The fields are uneven but it's easy to pick out a route to Ynysyfro golf course ahead. The signposts continue through the golf course and are somewhat helpful, although at one point a waymark leads into an impassable thicket, so the best advice is to stick as closely as possible to the woodland perimeter without trying to cut through it. When the tree line reaches the club house, cross safely over the green, with the club house on your right. The waymarks point into a small paddock but this requires crossing a deep, boggy ditch at the other side, so alternatively follow the road around until it rejoins the waymarked trail at a house. Leave the tarmac road and follow a track alongside the garden. The trail now joins a tarmac lane running back to Fourteen Locks, passing neatly between the Ynysyfro Reservoirs.

Back at the visitor centre, interpretation boards and intricately hand-painted maps show the Fourteen Locks as a vital cog in an integrated transport network. There was real drive and energy – and muscle power – to get the network of canals and tramroads up and running, and it could be argued that the Cefn Flight is as significant a piece of the jigsaw as landmark sites such as Blaenavon. The thought-provoking panels are reason enough to hang around the visitor centre for quite some time after your walk but, just in case you need another, there's also the Dadford Tearoom, serving the thickest, creamiest wedges of Victoria sponge imaginable at that peaceful canal-side patio.

The Fourteen Locks Visitor Centre car park is open between 6.30am and 4.45pm.

17. Caerleon and Chepstow Hill

Approximate distance	4 miles
Approximate time	2 hours
Starting point	Roman amphitheatre, Broadway Lane, Newport
Grading	A largely countryside walk with some steep climbs and spectacular views

With 2,000 years of history and said to be the first seat of King Arthur, Caerleon is a fascinating place on the banks of the River Usk. Starting and finishing at a Roman amphitheatre and following the route of a Roman road, this trail crams in a great deal, not only illustrating a rich story but showcasing stunning countryside views from Chepstow Hill.

Caerleon, a few miles north of Newport, was the headquarters of the 2nd Augustan Legion from AD75 until the end of the third century. Known as Isca, the fortress housed more than 5,000 soldiers brought to south Wales to tame the indigenous Silures, its location on the Usk a strategic master move. It was one of the most important military sites in Roman Britain; a thriving community of shops, baths and temples. Excitingly, our understanding of its prominence has been given a massive boost by recent excavations carried out by archaeology students and staff from Cardiff and other universities. Using geophysical equipment, they discovered a complex of large monumental buildings and a port outside the fortress, between the river and the amphitheatre. The buildings' size and design suggest administrative centres and markets – a Roman civic centre – while the port includes a main quay wall, wharves and landing stages. The excavations in Priory Field unearthed all sorts of metal, glass and pottery artefacts and attracted world-wide attention due to their significance.

The trail starts in the amphitheatre, one of several sites in the UK claimed as the site of the Round Table! Excavations in the 1920s revealed that the theatre was used not only for shows but also for training the troops garrisoned within the fortress. Today the arena is covered with grass but in the first century it would have been strewn with sand as a more suitable surface for the often violent spectacles which took place, watched by a crowd of up to 6,000. The stone wall running along the eastern edge of the field surrounded Isca. Initially these defences consisted of a turf-fronted clay bank dotted with timber palisades but they were strengthened in the early second century and the stone wall was built against the earthen ramparts.

Walk around the amphitheatre in a clockwise direction and through the gate in the far left hand corner. Walk across the next field, keeping to the left hand boundary wall, and over the stile in the corner into a third field. Note that the field to the left of this one is where the university excavations were carried out. Cross the field to the pavement and turn right on White Hart Lane, then right again into Caerleon Road. This is a busy main thoroughfare and although the bridge we need to cross is to the right, it might be wise to follow Caerleon Road to the left for a short distance to the crossing, doubling back on the other side.

A Roman re-enactment at Caerleon amphitheatre
Photo courtesy of Newport City Council

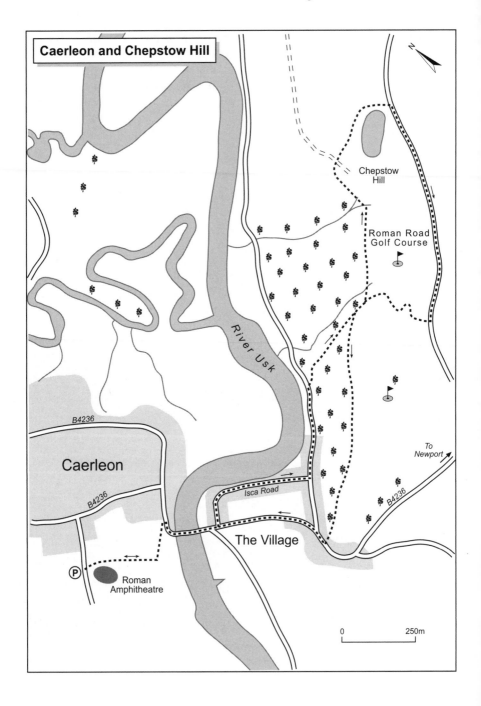

The trail crosses the stone bridge, built in the early 1800s to replace a wooden bridge which had stood for centuries. Turn left along New Road and quickly left again into Lulworth Road, signposted Usk Valley Walk. The street bends round into Isca Road, a pretty lane full of old cottages and character. One house, called the White Lion, was a 17th century inn serving this side of the original wooden crossing over the River Usk. Further along, at the head of Isca Road, is the Bell Inn, another pub from the same era and near to the site of a Roman burial ground.

Turn left in front of the Bell along Bulmore Road. When the road starts to dip downhill, the trail bears right onto the path signposted Usk Valley Walk. Climb the five steps, go over the stile and continue up the grassy path next to the fence. Reaching a kissing gate, the trail continues uphill to a gate on the left, where it bears right up some more steps. Through another kissing gate are more steps and soon after this comes a fork, at which the trail heads left, still following the Usk Valley Walk signs uphill.

Through the next gate the path reaches a golf course. Bear left up the grassy bank and walk along the perimeter of the course, keeping the wood on your left. This is the route of the old Roman road leading to Caerleon. At the top of the golf course is a tarmac road running horizontally; cross the road to reach the grass embankment overlooking the reservoir. This is the top of Chepstow Hill and the perfect point to stop for a picnic or simply a breather to take in the views. This south easterly corner of Wales unfurls and the Usk winds sleepily around the contours in its path below, the views proving that Wales can do gentle hills as beautifully as majestic mountains.

The trail continues clockwise along the embankment and around the reservoir until reaching Catsash Road, a narrow country lane, to the far right of the golf course. The trail turns right past the Celtic Manor Lodge, part of the sprawling resort which hosted the 2010 Ryder Cup. Newport's stake for the competition was viewed by some as a bold one but, in the context of the views behind us, certainly more than credible.

Catsash Road descends downhill, where shortly on the right, just below the first house, is a small gap in the hedge leading back into the golf course. Inside the course, head for the bench and turn right along the tarmac path. After 20m the trail veers left at the junction and winds down through the course (beware of golf balls whizzing past!). At the next fork turn right, cross over the tarmac and head towards the signpost ahead on the left. This brings you back to the gate into the wood where, rather than returning the way it came, the trail turns left at the fork, following the direction of the signs with a yellow arrow on a green background. The path reaches a wooden platform and goes up some steps, over a stile on the right and continues downhill. This stretch through the woods follows a narrow path and although it's a pleasant woodland walk it can be quite overgrown with nettles, so boots and trousers are a better option than walking sandals and shorts, even on warm days.

Eventually the path reaches three steps, followed quickly by another three onto New Road. Turn right and follow the road downhill, taking care as there is no pavement. Ahead is the junction of New Road and Lulworth Road, from where the trail returns over the bridge into Caerleon. It's a quick walk back to Broadway Lane car park but alternatively, carry on past

This sculpture on Isca Road is one of the Caerleon trail's many interesting features

White Hart Lane and to the junction of Castle Street and High Street. There is a multitude of historic buildings in Caerleon, including the Hanbury Arms, built by the wealthy Morgan family, and the remains of the castle. The castle tower was made almost entirely from stone 'recycled' from the Roman fortress – or 'mooted up' (stolen!) as the locals more bluntly termed it.

Caerleon town centre, particularly the High Street, is a quaint jumble of buildings from several periods, all piled up about each other. But perhaps the best way to bookend this walk is with another slice of Roman history. The National Roman Legion Museum on High Street explains how the Augustan Legion was such a formidable force, while exhibits such as intricate gemstones and daily utensils go some way to bringing colour to the Romans' personal lives. Also in the town are the Fortress Baths and the barracks, which complete our picture of the scale and determined efficiency of Isca.

18. Newport Chartists' Walk

Approximate distance	2 miles
Approximate time	1 hour
Starting point	St Woolos Hospital, Stow Hill
Grading	A mainly gentle city centre route but including the steep gradient of Stow Hill

The story of Chartism is embedded in Welsh history in the form of the Newport Rising of 1839. On November 4, more than 20 men in a 5,000-strong army of Chartists were shot dead in a street battle outside Newport's Westgate Hotel. The legacy of the Rising is still evident throughout the streets of Newport and this trail takes in some of the pivotal points where the drama unfolded, and where the event is still commemorated today.

The 1830s saw a growing movement across the UK for equity for the ordinary classes. The People's Charter, from which Chartism took its name, called for universal male suffrage at a time when less than one in eight men and certainly no women had the vote. Ballots weren't secret and the Charter was supported by many men who did have the vote, not just those who didn't. In Newport the movement was led by a man called John Frost, who had previously been the mayor of Newport but became increasingly radicalised. Chartism gathered pace in industrial valleys towns including Nantyglo, Blaenavon and Tredegar, and on the night of November 3 more than 5,000 coal and iron workers marched through the dark, reaching Newport just after 9am.

They were met at the Westgate Hotel by an army of soldiers and special constables amassed by mayor Thomas Phillips and were defeated in just 25 minutes. Depending on reports, the dead numbered between 22 and 28. Rape of the Fair Country *romanticises the Rising, ending with the deaths of some characters whilst hero Iestyn Mortymer is among the cartfuls of rebels heading to Monmouth for trial. John Frost and two other leaders, William Jones and Zephaniah Williams, were convicted of treason and sentenced to death, although this was commuted to transportation.*

The trail starts outside St Woolos Hospital on the busy Stow Hill. To the right of the hospital gates is a red brick building which in 1839 was the Union Workhouse, a grim destination for paupers and their families. Head in the other direction down Stow Hill, towards the city centre, and you will quickly come to St Woolos Square, one of the gathering points for Chartists trying to free comrades already imprisoned in the Westgate. The square stands at the entrance of St Woolos Cathedral, where in the churchyard are the unmarked graves of 10 dead Chartists. Today the square and cathedral are squeezed onto an island swamped by city life, encircled by traffic, shops and restaurants. But within the churchyard, under the enormous mature trees brushing the cathedral tower, is a sense of calm in the wake of the site's turbulent history.

Stow Hill follows the curve of the churchyard and descends sharply towards the city centre past the Church House restaurant, once the site of the Six Bells pub and another rallying point for protestors. As Stow Hill bends around to the left, a lane on the right hand corner gives a clear view in the distance of the Grade I-listed Newport Transporter Bridge. Immediately past the lane a white terrace sits awkwardly in the cramped bend of the road; in the 1830s these cottages each slept up to 20 people, epitomising the harsh working lives of ordinary men attracted to the Chartist cause in the belief that the vote would bring about improvements.

The trail plunges down Stow Hill and past the grand St Mary's Church on the right. On the left is the site of the Mayor's House, now

Chartist sculptures outside the Westgate Hotel

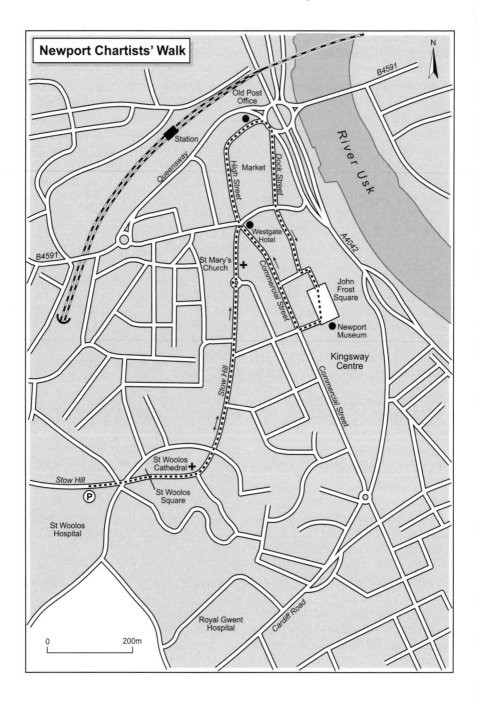

a betting shop. Thomas Phillips lived here in 1839 and spent the night of November 3 just yards away in the Westgate Hotel, 5,000 Chartists marching towards him. In the morning a band of soldiers joined him, hiding behind the shutters ready to open fire. The back of the Westgate is at the base of Stow Hill, while its front entrance is around to the right on Commercial Street. Today it is reduced to a sorry shadow of its former stature but the junction is enlivened by a cluster of Chartist sculptures and it's an evocative place to imagine the chaos as men lay dying in the street. The youngest to die, 19-year-old George Shell, lay bleeding for hours while the soldiers prevented supporters from giving him even a sip of water. Shell, a carpenter among the first to sign the Charter at Pontypool, had written a letter to his parents before the march, which was later produced in evidence against the Chartists to show intent of treason.

From the junction, walk up High Street to the Old Post Office, the site of the birthplace of John Frost. Thomas Street, where he was born, has long been demolished but a plaque marks the location. Outside the Old Post Office is a recreation of the Newport Cross, part of a medieval cross unearthed by workmen digging the foundations for Newport Bridge in 1925. The original is on display at Newport Museum. Interestingly the Old Post Office building once housed the town's first telephone exchange, known then as the Savoy.

From here continue to the end of High Street, where Newport Castle can be glimpsed across the busy junction. Turn right into Dock Street and past the Victorian Provisions Market on the right. At the fork take the right hand street up to a sculpture of a bull, entitled The Vision of St Gwynllyw. Turn left and into the pedestrian tunnel, where the Chartists' Mural runs the full length of one wall. It's a beautiful mosaic piece depicting the march and the bloody battle, with the Six Points of the Charter incorporated into the protestors' banners. Five of these points are today enshrined in the UK constitution, a sign of the rights we now perhaps take for granted.

The tunnel opens onto John Frost Square. After Frost's sentencing, more than three million people signed a petition for clemency and he was transported to what we now know as Tasmania, returning to Britain in 1854. He was pardoned two years later and died in Bristol. Like the Westgate Hotel, the Square now looks a little forlorn but it has been earmarked for redevelopment, as befits the site of Newport Museum and

The story of the Rising is told in the Chartists' Mural at John Frost Square

Art Gallery and library on the far side of the Square. Newport Tourist Information Centre is also here, with plenty of pointers to other Chartist sites in south east Wales.

John Frost Square is the end of the Chartists' Walk. To get back to the starting point, follow Llanarth Street, which is to the right of the library, to Commercial Street. Turn right to return to the Westgate Hotel and the junction of Stow Hill.

19. Cardiff Centenary Walk

Approximate distance	2½ miles
Approximate time	1½ hours
Starting point	The Old Library, Working Street
Grading	A level trail through the heart of Cardiff. This walk will take much longer than the estimated time if long stops are made at every landmark

The Centenary Walk is one of the best ways to understand the rich layers of Cardiff's history. Elevated to city status in 1905, Cardiff marked its centenary year in 2005 and is a compact but worthy capital; diverse and exciting. It also has swathes of green space, giving it a cleaner and more spacious appeal than some cities. The route described here is a version of a celebratory walk created by Cardiff Council in 2005 but it's been slightly abbreviated, partly due to extensive redevelopment in the heart of the shopping centre and partly because Cardiff's historic landmarks are too numerous to list fully here.

The history of Cardiff dates back 2,000 years, to a Roman settlement constructed on the site of the present castle. With William the Conqueror's victory, in marched the Normans and in medieval times Cardiff was a significant port. By Tudor times, it was established as a structured, settled town with a population of between 1,500 to 2,000. At the end of the reign of Elizabeth I, the view of Cardiff would have been an interesting jumble of merchants' houses crowded into a criss-cross of narrow streets. Cardiff historian Jim Cowan gives award-winning tours covering sections of the Centenary Walk, leaving visitors with evocative and amusing impressions of houses teetering upwards closer and closer to their neighbours, upper storeys overhanging the lower floors to reduce tax, which was based on ground-floor footprint.

The trail starts at the Old Library in Working Street, which now accommodates the glass-fronted Cardiff Tourist Information Centre and

The Cardiff Story museum. Original features have been beautifully preserved to give an idea of how the 'Free Library, Museum and School of Arts' looked when it opened in 1882. Cardiff was one of the last cities to emerge from the industrial revolution and was generally thought to be less grand than, say, Manchester and Liverpool, which had been flourishing for generations. By the 1880s Cardiff was catching up in terms of public buildings, although the library was nevertheless considered modest by the

The Old Library and St John's Church, Cardiff

standards of the day. Initially the library's design allowed men and women to mix, but this caused such a scandal that a separate entrance was built for women. This tiled corridor today looks spectacular, but in fact it was ordered from the catalogue of the largest tile manufacturer in the UK! The Prince of Wales, the future King Edward VII, opened an extension to the building in 1896 and later an avenue was named after him in Cathays Park.

Facing the Old Library's front entrance, turn left towards the Hayes. 'Hayes' was the Norman word for a plot of land enclosed by hedges, and these allotments were where local people grew their vegetables. The Hayes Island Snack Bar in the middle of the square is a well-known landmark and if it reminds you of a train station, that's because it used to be the Tramway Parcel Express Office! The area to the left of the Hayes has been transformed to accommodate the second phase of the St David's shopping centre. At the end of the Hayes, on the right, is the Tabernacl Chapel, a Welsh language chapel which hosted the first *Songs of Praise* broadcast in 1961. Ahead is Mill Lane, which follows the route of the Glamorganshire Canal.

Just before Mill Lane turn right into Caroline Street and pass the Brewery Quarter, another new development on a site known for ale-brewing since the early 18th century. At the end of Caroline Street turn right and follow St Mary Street, looking out for the grand Royal Hotel on the corner opposite. This was where Captain Robert Scott and his men dined the night before the *Terra Nova* set sail to the Antarctic from Cardiff Docks. Outside the hotel is the glass-encased Pierhead Clock, which began life at the Pierhead Building in Cardiff Bay in 1897 and has recently been restored and incorporated into a piece of street artwork here.

The Centenary Walk continues down St Mary St past the Royal and Morgan Arcades, two of the city's network of Victorian arcades renowned for their eclectic boutiques and independent shops. These parallel arcades until recently flanked David Morgan, a popular department store which opened as a haberdasher's in 1879. David Morgan came up against 'the Courts', a labyrinth of cram-packed slums incubating mass outbreaks of typhus and cholera. In the 1840s Cardiff's population exploded with the opening of Bute Docks, a socially disastrous expansion as the right infrastructure wasn't in place to cope with the influx. David Morgan's solution was to buy up the Courts and gradually turn them into a shopping district, resulting in the arcades' higgledy-piggledy structure.

Past the Morgan Arcade, turn right into Wharton Street, which runs alongside Howells. James Howells was Cardiff's other retail magnate, opening his department store in 1865. Howells incorporates into its infrastructure some of the walls of the old Bethany Chapel, and a significant feature on one of the interior walls is a plaque commemorating Rawlins White, a Protestant fisherman from Bristol who was burned in Cardiff by Queen Mary.

At the end of Wharton Street, turn left into Trinity Street, where you will pass the rear entrance of the Old Library on your right and the Victorian market on your left. Cardiff Market is partly on the site of the county gaol and gallows, where martyr Dic Penderyn was hanged on August 13 1831 for his alleged role in the Merthyr Rising, detailed further in Walk 7. Directly ahead is St John's Church, the city centre's oldest church. Founded in Norman times, it was rebuilt in 1473 with a surprisingly elegant tower for a relatively small church. It was not the main church but a chapel of ease for St Mary's, although when this was destroyed in the floods of 1607 St John's became the parish church.

Inside the church is a memorial to Sir John Herbert, private secretary to Elizabeth 1 and James 1. Sir John and his brother, Sir William, controlled Cardiff during this time, although they were like chalk and cheese. Sir

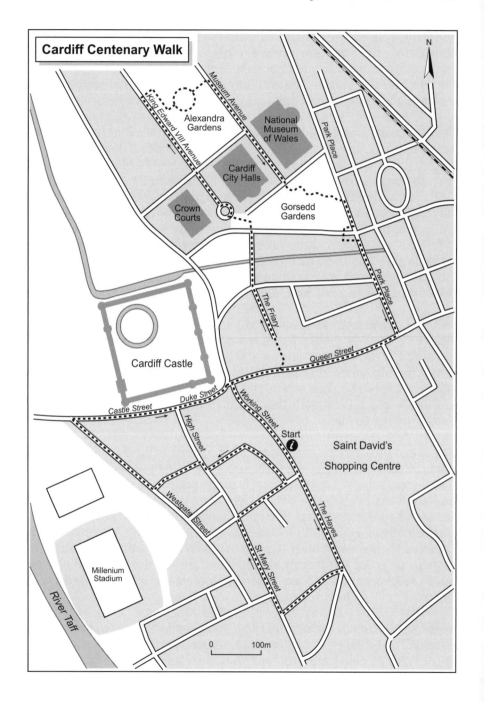

John trained as a lawyer and was the MP for Glamorgan; as a member of the Privy Council he was tipped to replace William Cecil as Secretary of State although in the event this position went to Cecil's son. Sir William, in contrast, was a rogue; essentially a gang leader in cahoots with the criminals and pirates for which Cardiff was notorious. Despite his dealings, Sir William never landed up in gaol – as also he happened to be a local Justice of the Peace! St John's also has beautiful stained glass, funded by the rich Bute family and including pieces by William Morris. Visitors receive a genuine welcome but should observe the custom of making a small donation in return for a look around.

From the church's main entrance, walk straight ahead into Church Street, passing the Old Arcade pub on the left. At the end of the street is the point where St Mary Street to the left seamlessly merges into High Street to the right. This road was the centre of the medieval town and annual fairs were held in front of the Guildhall in High Street, which was also used as a courtroom and had outside a whipping post, used as punishment for vagrancy. The buildings on St Mary Street and High Street are largely Victorian in their facades, highlighting Cardiff's burgeoning profile during the 19th century.

Cross the road and continue into Quay Street almost directly ahead. The River Taff used to reach Quay Street's junction with Westgate Street, often overflowing into it. However the curve of the river got in the way of the South Wales Railway, an extension of the Great Western Railway masterminded by Brunel, whose solution was simply to re-channel the river! Quay Street is also the point of the great flood which demolished St Mary's Church, surging up from the Bristol Channel and killing 2,000 people on its way, including many in Cardiff.

The end of Quay Street is the site of Blount's (pronounced Blunt's) Gate, the town's fifth gate after the north, south, east and west entrances. Originally called Wales Gate, it was renamed after a former gatekeeper and provided access to the River Taff from St Mary Street. Due to its inland waterways, Cardiff was a haven for pirates and had a reputation for lawlessness – an ironic tag given that a person could be hanged for stealing more than five shillings when the law was applied! Demolished in 1785, Blount's Gate is now commemorated by a blue plaque on the car park wall.

Slightly to the left is the home of Welsh rugby, the iconic Millennium Stadium. Turn right and follow Westgate Street to the Angel Hotel at the end, passing on the left the Millennium Stadium's predecessor, Cardiff Arms Park. At the Angel cross Castle Street and continue to the right, alongside the famous Animal Wall encircling the castle grounds. The hand-carved stone figures were designed by William Burges, the architect behind Cardiff Castle's Victorian apartments. The wall was originally built in front of the castle but was moved when the road was widened in 1925.

We're now at the entrance to Cardiff Castle, with millennia of history to peel away. The castle walls are a Victorian recreation of Roman walls, a romantic tribute to its origins as a fort constructed in around AD50. For centuries, this Roman past remained buried under mounds of earth added by the Normans but, in 1888, when the 3rd Marquess of Bute commissioned a new east tower, the early foundations were discovered. Lord Bute abandoned his plans for the tower, instead excavating the Roman ruins and gradually rebuilding walls on the original stonework. His reconstruction included a passageway with a dual purpose; it not only acted as a viewing gallery but allowed Lord Bute to take his daily walk

Roman meets Victorian history at Cardiff Castle
Photo courtesy of www.visitcardiff.com

even in bad weather! The gallery was later used as an air raid shelter during World War II.

The Butes were fabulously wealthy, their empire built on their ownership of the wasteland that was to become Cardiff Docks, from where millions of tons of Welsh coal were exported. The family had the castle mansion rebuilt in the 1770s but it was the 3rd Marquess, a shy scholar with a passion for history and archaeology, who transformed it into the Gothic fairytale standing today. He employed Burges to design a series of astonishingly opulent rooms, matched in their fantastical beauty by a sister creation, Castell Coch, a few miles north. Today Cardiff Castle is one of Wales' most-visited landmarks, with guided and audio tours in multiple languages and popular events such as public banquets in the undercroft.

Continue past the castle along Duke Street, whose name has nothing to do with the peerage but derives from Duck Street, as this was where poulterers sold their goods. At the far corner of the castle walls one of the few remaining sections of the old town wall is visible, prettily incorporated into a flower bed. Ahead is the now-pedestrianised Queen Street, which used to be Crockherbton Street but which was re-named in 1887 to mark Queen Victoria's Golden Jubilee. The trail follows Queen Street a little way, past the statue of Aneurin Bevan – who warrants a trail of his very own in Walk 9 – and turns left into The Friary, where the East Gate used to stand. In 1280, Franciscan Friars founded a friary on the spot now occupied by the tower block. Greyfriars Road, at the head of The Friary, gained its name from the grey habits the friars wore.

Cross Greyfriars Road, walking past Friary Gardens on the left. Below here was a dock feeder for the Glamorganshire Canal, which ran for 25 miles from Cyfarthfa in Merthyr to the docks. The dock feeder was cut in the 1830s to help flush mud and rubbish out of the canal. The canal, which had 52 locks, fell victim to the success of the Taff Vale Railway and the last barge passed along it in 1942.

Walk through the underpass and up into Cathays Park, one of the most impressive civic centres in Britain. To the right is City Hall, opened at a cost of £129,000 the year after Cardiff was granted city status. City Hall is defined by its 60-metre domed clock tower, although equally as splendid is the interior, which can be viewed by the public when functions

Cardiff City Hall fronts one of the most impressive civic centres in Britain
Photo courtesy of www.visitcardiff.com

and meetings aren't taking place. In the middle of the road outside City Hall an ornate turning circle honours the Welshmen who died in the Boar War at the turn of the century.

To the left of City Hall is King Edward VII Avenue. Follow this past the law courts on the left to the first building in Cathays Park to be completed, the classical University of Wales Registry. A little further along is the Glamorgan Building, now part of Cardiff University, and then the Bute Building, architect Percy Thomas' first major project. From here enter Alexandra Garden and turn right past the Falklands Memorial. Just beyond this is the Welsh National War Memorial to the soldiers of World War I, its ring of Corinthian columns encircling a fountain and three bronze figures.

Exiting Alexandra Gardens on the far side, follow Museum Avenue to the right, back in the direction of the city centre. In front of the National Museum of Wales is Gorsedd Gardens, home of the Gorsedd circle of stones which marked the 1899 National Eisteddfod and which were moved here in 1905. Cross through the park diagonally to the left and exit opposite the stunning Park House, designed by Burges and with plenty of his signature stonework evident.

At the traffic lights cross the busy Boulevard de Nantes and follow Park Place, passing the Edwardian, reputedly haunted New Theatre on your right and the Parc Hotel by Thistle on your left. From here, turn right and follow Queen Street back to its junction with Duke Street. Turn left into Working Street and back towards the Old Library. On the way you will pass the Owain Glyndŵr pub, named after the self-proclaimed Prince of Wales. Glyndŵr started as a loyal supporter of the English but fell out with the supporters of Henry IV and was crowned Prince of Wales in 1400. In 1404 he attacked the walled settlement at Cardiff, causing widespread fire. The Owain Glyndŵr pub stands on the spot of one of the oldest inns in Cardiff, known in the 1730s as the Mapley Arms. Other reincarnations include the Tennis Court, due to the real tennis court which used to stand behind it and, in the 1970s, the Buccaneer, after infamous Llanrumney pirate Captain Henry Morgan.

20. Cardiff Bay Heritage Trail

Approximate distance	4 miles
Approximate time	2 hours
Starting point	Roald Dahl Plass, Cardiff Bay
Grading	A gentle, flat trail around Cardiff Bay via the renowned Cardiff Bay Barrage and Penarth Marina

If the story of coal and iron started in the heart of the valleys, the sweeping curve of Cardiff Bay is where its journey in Wales ended. The Bay – then simply known as Cardiff Docks – was once one of the busiest coal ports in the world and gave the 3rd Marquess of Bute the reputation of the richest man in Britain. With the decline of the coalfields in the 20th century the site became almost derelict, but the creation of the Cardiff Bay Barrage has regenerated the area almost beyond recognition and it's now one of Wales' most beloved tourist hotspots.

Originally wetlands owned by the 2nd Marquess, John Crichton-Stuart, the land was transformed by the opening of West Bute Dock in 1839. Although the Butes were central figures – and certainly the main profiteers – they are far from the only colourful characters in the Bay's rich history. This family-friendly trail explores Cardiff's links with Antarctic hero Captain Scott and children's author Roald Dahl, as well showcasing flagship TV. World-famous shows such as Torchwood *and* Doctor Who *are filmed in the Bay, while the recent creation of the Roath Lock drama village has given* Casualty *and Welsh language programmes a home here too.*

For much of the way the trail follows the Cardiff Bay Trail and is therefore not only very well signposted but also accessible for wheelchairs and pushchairs. The trail starts at the Water Tower, an impressive 70ft glass structure with rivulets of water streaming constantly within and instantly recognisable to *Torchwood* fans as one of the show's iconic landmarks. The Water Tower stands outside the beautiful Wales Millennium Centre in

Wales Millennium Centre and the Water Tower are at the heart of vibrant Cardiff Bay
Photo courtesy of www.visitcardiff.com

Roald Dahl Plass, an amphitheatre formerly known as the Oval Basin, which neighbours a lively blend of cafes, restaurants and bars.

Standing at the Water Tower and facing the Bay, follow the waterfront around to the left, passing the stunning Victorian redbrick Pierhead Building, originally the home of the Cardiff Railway Company. Next door is the imposing slate, glass and wood structure of the Senedd, the home of the National Assembly for Wales. Designed to make the democratic process as transparent as possible, it's an open building and visitors can view the Chamber from a public gallery on an upper level.

From the Senedd continue clockwise towards the whitewashed Norwegian Church. This picture-postcard church was transported to Cardiff in the 1860s to cater for the Scandinavian seafarers visiting the docks, and was later the baptism church of Roald Dahl, who was born in Llandaff, north Cardiff, to Norwegian parents. Dahl lived in Cardiff throughout his childhood before creating some of fiction's best-loved – and most vile – characters, including *The Twits* and *The BFG*.

In front of the church is the Captain Scott Memorial, a mosaic statue overlooking the spot from which Scott's ship, the *Terra Nova*, sailed to the Antarctic in 1910. Huge amounts of money were raised by Cardiff industrialists and ship owners to fund the voyage, and thousands of well-wishers crowded into Roath Dock and along Penarth Head to see the ship set sail. But the euphoria turned to tragedy, with the five-strong British Antarctic Expedition team perishing and the *Terra Nova* forlornly returning to Cardiff nearly three years to the day after she sailed amid such joyful scenes. An outdoor exhibition on Captain Scott's journey is displayed further along the trail under the barrage sails.

From the mosaic statue the trail crosses a striking new bridge across the waterway into Roath Basin and follows the curve of the Bay towards the barrage. It's a particularly popular path and on warm weekends can be bustling. Soon the trail arrives at a children's play area and a lively skate park, near which are interesting interpretation boards revealing facets about life at the coal face. From here the trail begins to cross the barrage, an 800m embankment which has created a huge freshwater bay. About halfway across are the impressive barrage sails and views across the channel to Somerset, with the islands of Flatholm and Steepholm in between. At the end of the barrage are the three locks, a good spot at

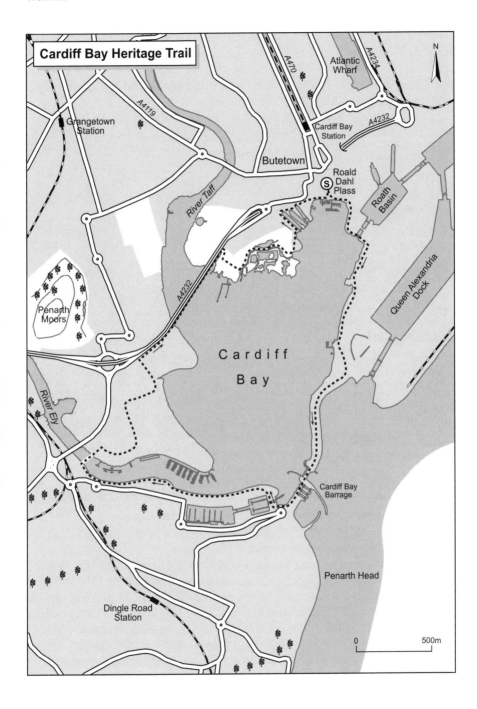

Cardiff Bay Heritage Trail

which to watch the boats coming in and out of the Bay, no matter how low the tide. The nuts and bolts of the barrage aren't always pretty and its creation caused years of controversy over the potential damage to wildlife, yet there's no doubt the daily workings of the bridge make an impressive sight in a spectacular environment.

Cardiff Bay has been transformed into a major tourism attraction
Photo courtesy of www.visitcardiff.com

From the barrage the trail lands at Penarth Head opposite the grand, yellow-brick Custom House. Now a restaurant, it was built in 1865 to allow officials to control imports and exports into the Port of Cardiff. Penarth benefited from Cardiff's fortunes as the main satellite town and is still a sought-after location today thanks to its marina developments and stunning coastal views. The trail now dips into one of those developments, running from the Custom House along Penarth Portway. At the mini-roundabout turn immediately right and follow the marina waterfront around to the left past the marina offices. Cross the small lock gates, from where you can follow the waterfront and the River Ely almost to Pont y Werin bridge. When the path ends, turn left onto Marconi Avenue and follow the road to the mini roundabout flanked by a restaurant and supermarket. Just past this roundabout the trail runs along the water's edge to Pont y Werin, a 140m-bridge providing a cycle and pedestrian link between Penarth and the International Sports Village, another major investment in the Bay's development. It's a pretty sight at night time, rows of lights sparkling along the length of the railings.

Across Pont y Werin, turn right along Watkiss Way, passing Cardiff International White Water centre. The trail then takes a left into Olympian Drive, opposite the gleaming blue structure of Cardiff International Pool, then right into International Drive. This area is another site which has undergone a fascinating transformation from forgotten wasteland to energetic visitor zone, although locally-loved historic landmarks did pay the price. At the end of International Drive turn left onto Ferry Road, following the blue signs towards the dual carriageway bridge. Immediately this side of the bridge, on the right, is a ramp-like path signposted Mermaid Quay, which leads onto a broad pedestrian path alongside the A4232. The dual carriageway is noisy but the walking and cycling route is dedicated and users are entertained at one point by a sculpture of a man peering into a giant, shiny sphere.

Immediately at the far end of the bridge, turn right at the gantry and walk down towards the Cardiff Yacht Club and the wetland area, where you can learn more about some of the wildlife inhabiting Cardiff Bay. Follow the path to the left through the wetlands and up to the right, towards the group of bronze curlews. Ahead is the five-star St David's Hotel and Spa, with its spectacular roof. Follow the boardwalk around the hotel, almost at water level, and towards Techniquest. From here the trail passes the former Pilotage Office, which was built as a stable in the 1860s and is now a brasserie, and heads through the pedestrianised area. It's now a quick stroll along the waterfront back to your starting point in Roald Dahl Plass, passing as you go a bronze sculpture of a young couple – plus an irresistible string of ice cream parlours.

Bibliography

The Welsh Academy Encyclopaedia of Wales: John Davies, Nigel Jenkins, Menna Baines and Peredur I. Lynch

The Making of Wales: John Davies

Aneurin Bevan (Vols I and II): Michael Foot

Aneurin Bevan: Brome Vincent

Building for a Better Future; The Brynmawr Rubber Factory: Victoria Perry

The Essential Cardiff Castle: Matthew Williams

Big Pit, National Coal Museum – A Guide: Sharon Ford, Ceri Thompson and Peter Walker

Llantrisant from Old Photographs: Dean Powell

Also available from Sigma

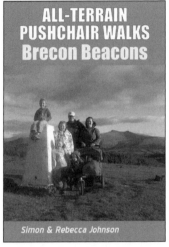

ALL-TERRAIN PUSHCHAIR WALKS IN THE BRECON BEACONS
Simon & Rebecca Johnson
This book is written for families wanting to take their children walking using All Terrain Pushchairs (ATPs) on beautiful walks in the Brecon Beacons National Park. The 30 walks are also suitable for families without ATPs and anyone wishing to enjoy a walk without too much gradient and few if any stiles. The paths are suitable for double ATPs, as the authors have walked them all with their own children. Above all, get out into the wonderful, easily accessible Brecon Beacons, and enjoy the beauty, the nature and the tranquillity of this Welsh National Park.
£8.99

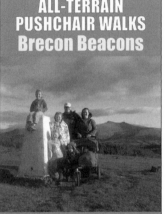

NORTH WALES WALKING
on the level
Norman & June Buckley
This is the seventh volume of the popular and well-established series of 'level walks' books. There are 30 walks covering an area from The Great Orme to Cemlyn Bay. Whilst walks in North Wales are treasured by those who love the mountains, the balance of the book is much enhanced by the inclusion of the Conwy Valley and the Lleyn Peninsula, both part of the wider definition of Snowdonia, and by Anglesey, its near neighbour.
£8.99

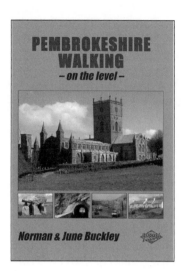

PEMBROKESHIRE WALKING ON THE LEVEL
Norman & June Buckley
This is the sixth volume of the popular and well-established series of 'level walks' books. Discover both the breath-taking splendour of the Pembrokeshire coast and its diverse inland landscape. The 25 comparatively short, easy walks in this book include clear route directions, map and a brief description of features encountered along the way as well as recommendations for refreshment. £8.99

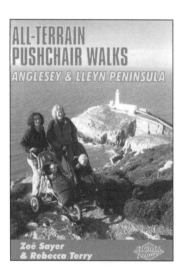

ALL-TERRAIN PUSHCHAIR WALKS: ANGLESEY & LLEYN PENINSULA
Zoë Sayer & Rebecca Terry
Pushchair walks by the sea — from beach strolls to cliff-top rambles. There are 30 tried-and-tested routes from simple beach strolls to rugged inland hill-top rambles through fields, woods and over hills and mountains with scarcely any obstacles and never any need to remove the child from the pushchair. £7.95

WALKS IN THE FOREST OF DEAN AND WYE VALLEY
Dave Meredith

The Forest of Dean and Wye Valley is a paradise for both the keen rambler and the casual stroller. The 22 walks described in this book are along easy footpaths taking you to spectacular viewpoints, along woodland glades carpeted with bluebells, daffodils and foxgloves, and under the dappled shade of its golden autumn canopy. £8.99

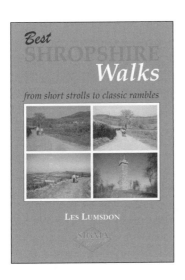

BEST SHROPSHIRE WALKS 2ND EDITION
From short strolls to classic rambles
Les Lumsdon

A new revised edition of this much loved guide contains 36 walks, including 12 completely new routes, located in all parts of the county. Several walks feature fine hill walking on the Welsh borders and others start from delightful villages and hamlets in the north and east of the county.

The Shropshire countryside really comes alive in this well-researched book. All of the walks include stories about the locality: folklore and legends, attractions and facilities. There are clear maps and a selection of photographs to make for an enjoyable and informative read. £8.99

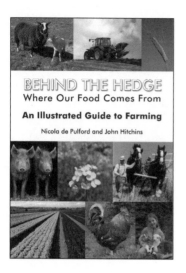

BEHIND THE HEDGE
Where Our Food Comes From
An Illustrated Guide to Farming
Nicola de Pulford & John Hithins
Behind the Hedge is for everyone who wants to know more about the food we eat, the land it is grown and reared on, and those who farm it. It is an easy-to-follow guide which will help you identify in their natural environment our crops, fruit and farm animals, agricultural buildings and machinery, the farming landscape and the wildlife it supports.

Never again will you mistake a field of wheat for one of barley, or an Aberdeen Angus cow for a Hereford. By dipping in and out of this beautifully illustrated book, you will learn to recognise the crops, farm animals and wildlife on the other side of the hedge.
£12.99

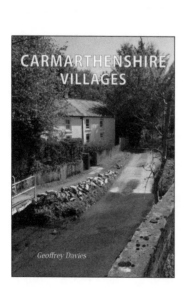

CARMARTHENSHIRE VILLAGES
Geoffrey Davies
Carmarthenshire is one of the most beautiful counties in Britain, yet is often overlooked by the tourist racing towards the beaches of Pembrokeshire. It is essentially a rural county with the majority of the population living in villages and smaller communities. There is ample evidence of pre Roman settlement in the county and many villages have their origins in the Dark Ages, before written documentation.
The aim of this book is to give a guide to the county's smaller communities, with a brief description, a little history and some stories of village characters.
£8.99